Pathways
to
Responsibility

Pathways
to
Responsibility

A Responsibility, Character Education, and Violence Prevention Curriculum for Grade Two

Donnita Weddle and Marian Adams

Learning Publications, Inc.
Holmes Beach, Florida

ISBN 1-55691-213-7

Learning Publications, Inc.
5351 Gulf Drive
P.O. Box 1338
Holmes Beach, FL 34218-1338

Printing: 5 4 3 2 1   Year: 06 05 04 03 02

Printed in the United States of America

Contents

Our Promise to You xi

Animal Characters Greet You xii

Responsibility

Lesson 1 -To Be Responsible.. 1

Lesson 2 - Responsibility Is Important 6

Being Special

Lesson 3 - I Am Special 9

Kindness and Cooperation

Lesson 4 - Cooperation 14

Lesson 5 - Kindness 19

Lesson 6 - Honesty... 23

Lesson 7 - Respect 27

Self-Control

Lesson 8 - Self-Control 30

Lesson 9 - Anger Management 34

Problem Solving

Lesson 10 - "I" Messages... 39

Lesson 11 - Seeing Both Sides... 42

Lesson 12 - Resolving Conflicts Peacefully 47

Empathy

Lesson 13- Being a Good Friend 52

Lesson 14 - Listening Is Important 56

Lesson 15 - Playing Fair 61

Lesson 16 - Feeling Left Out 65

Coping

Lesson 17 - Handling Bullies... 68

Lesson 18 - Handling Put-Downs 72

Lesson 19 - Refusal Skills.. 76

Decision Making

Lesson 20 - Making Good Choices 81

Lesson 21 - Learning from Our Mistakes 85

Drugs and Alcohol

Lesson 22 - Smoking Is Harmful 89

Lesson 23 - Alcohol Causes Problems 94

Lesson 24 - Drugs Are Dangerous 99

Goal Setting

Lesson 25 - Setting Goals 103

Appendices

Appendix A – How to Make Sock Puppets 106

Appendix B – Resource Sheets 108

Appendix C – Student Responsibility Contract 112

Acknowledgments

Thanks to Donnita's daughter, Kimberly Eileen Weddle, for giving encouragement to meet the challenge and accomplish the goal of writing this curriculum.

Thanks to Stan Davis, Sunnyside School District, Sunnyside, Wash., for his trust and belief that helped cultivate the education, experience, and confidence that made the creation of this curriculum possible.

Thanks to the students of Lapwai Elementary, Lapwai, Ida.; Sunnyside School District, Sunnyside, Wash.; Culdesac School District, Culdesac, Ida.; Sacajawea Junior High and Lewiston High School, Lewiston, Ida. Through their participation they contributed to the creation of this curriculum.

Special thanks to friend and professional artist Bill Schreib who took our concepts of the Sunshine Elementary characters and made them real.

About the Authors

This responsibility, character education, and violence curriculum was written by Donnita Weddle, M.S.ED/Counseling, B.S. Elementary ED, B.S. Criminal Corrections, A.A. in Behavioral Science, and Marian Adams, A.A. and B.A. English/journalism with history, social studies, and reading additional certification, Teacher of the Year 1991 and Lewiston City Commission member for Public Education Government Channel 13. The purpose of the curriculum is to have combined in one book for each grade level many of the techniques for teaching awareness and skills to promote responsible behavior in young children.

When Donnita Weddle, a teacher and counselor for many years, researched a responsibility and violence prevention curriculum for classroom guidance, she found she had to go to dozens of sources to put together a complete set of the teaching materials. This brought about the awareness of a need for one resource that would cover all aspects of responsibility, character education, and violence prevention. In addition to counseling and teaching in these areas, Ms. Weddle has helped various schools set up playground conflict-management programs by training students and staff in the skills needed for peer mediation. Because of her expertise, she was invited to publish an article on the subject in the *Washington Learner* in 1994.

Marian Adams has been a journalism and English secondary teacher for 21 years and was aware of the need for students to learn responsibility, character education, and violence prevention at a young age so they may practice it in the teenage years. She has also traveled to England, China, and Germany observing education methods in those countries and lecturing on American journalism education.

Ms. Weddle, with her very specific ideas about lesson content, and Ms. Adams, with her writing skills and creative insights, teamed up to write this terrific, user-friendly curriculum.

The goal of publishing these materials is to help educators teach the important skills to increase responsible behavior in as many elementary school-age children as possible. The plan is to continue the focus on responsibility, character education, and violence prevention in the secondary school area with a curriculum for teenagers.

Our Promise to You

We agree with parents, teachers, counselors, and administrators — children are special! Children need to be cherished and loved but they also need to learn to grow up to be responsible adults. We give you our promise that you can help children to learn to cope with the feelings and problems all of us must face in this modern world while still nurturing their fragile psyches and creative spirits. If we, with your help, can get across to the child the 10 principles of being responsible adults, then we will have given our children a truly great gift. The child needs to feel and act with the following principles as their guide to life:

1. I am special.
2. Everyone is special and I respect everyone.
3. I am a good listener and have empathy.
4. I am honest.
5. I can make good decisions.
6. I can solve problems without violence.
7. I set goals.
8. Although it is not always easy, I can cope with whatever I need to cope with.
9. Although I make mistakes, I am willing to learn.
10. I am responsible for my own actions.

The formative years are important. Preschool and primary children need to get a good base in living, feeling, and believing all 10 of these principles. We, as teachers, must always remember in the teaching of these principles that in the creative child is often the dream and innovation for the future.

One of the best ways for young children to learn these principles is by seeing examples of them being used. Parents and teachers should provide the examples by their words and actions. This is not always possible. Therefore, the school must reinforce and teach these principles.

To help teachers teach these principles, this primary-grade curriculum on responsibility, character education, and violence prevention has been prepared. It contains stories and activities for children in second grade.

Animal Characters Greet You

Setting: Anytown, USA ; Sunshine Elementary School

Characters:

- Lilly Lambkin – White, woolly lamb, a main character, twin to brother Lucky
- Lucky Lambkin – Black, woolly lamb, main character, twin to sister Lilly
- Ronnie Rabbit – Helpful black and white floppy-earred rabbit
- Susie Squirrel – Curious, brown, happy squirrel
- Doolee Dog – Full of mischief, somewhat of a bully
- Daisy Dog – Doolee's younger sister
- Cherry Chicken – Cheerleader type, happy and outgoing
- Ted Turkey – Funloving but likes to learn
- Minnie Moo – Shy and reserved
- Mabell Moo – Minnie's big sister who helps care for Minnie
- Corky Colt – High-spirited and full of fun
- Kathy Kat – Sympathetic, cares about others
- Billy Goat – A bit of a bully
- Polly Pigeon – New girl who is shy
- Bart Bull – Sixth-grade bully
- Vicki Vulture – New student who comes from the south and talks differently
- Gordy Goat – Billy's older brother
- Tony and Jack – Fifth graders who tried smoking and tried to talk the second graders into doing it

Adults:

- Teacher Mrs. Giraffe – Kind, considerate, knowledgeable, wise second-grade teacher of Lilly's class
- Teacher Mr. Moose – Enjoys children, kind, knowledgeable, likes second graders, teaches Lucky's class
- Various mothers as needed

Animal Characters Greet You at Sunshine Elementary Second Grade

Lilly Lambkin

Lucky Lambkin

Susie Squirrel

Doolee Dog

Daisy Dog

Cherry Chicken

Ted Turkey

Minnie Moo

Mabell Moo

Corky Colt

Kathy Kat

Billy Goat

Polly Pigeon

Bart Bull

Gordy Goat

Ronnie Rabbit

Vicki Vulture

Tony & Jack

Adult Teachers:

Mrs. Giraffe

Mr. Moose

☑ Lesson 1
To Be Responsible

> To Be Responsible – To be responsible means to accept the obligation to be accountable, dependable, and trustworthy.

Being responsible means to be accountable for our own actions and take charge of our own lives. Others will trust us and rely on us when we take responsibility for our school assignments, our chores at home and our relationships with friends. When we complete our school assignments and do our chores, we are accountable and dependable. When we treat our friends well and keep our promises, we are trustworthy. Being responsible for our actions isn't always easy. Sometimes we have to work at it but it is very important as we grow up. When we practice responsible behavior, we feel good about ourselves.

Instructions: Tell the students that we are going to begin a series of lessons that will teach us about being responsible in many areas of our lives. In these lessons we will meet many interesting characters who will be learning these lessons along with us as they attend the second grade at Sunshine Elementary school in Anytown, U.S.A. We will have many exciting adventures with these warm, lovable students who do many of the same things we do and face many of the same problems we have. Since they are not always perfect and neither are we, we will find out how they handle various situations and learn to be responsible.

Characters: Introduce all the characters to the students. Show pictures of the characters when describing them. In this lesson, Lucky Lambkin learns about responsibility with his friend Corky Colt. Funloving friends Billy Goat and Ted Turkey play with them in the park. If intending to make puppets, now would be the time to have a work session to make all the puppets. (See instructions for Making Sock Puppets in Appendix A).

Directions – Explain the use of character puppets. Discuss the introduction and briefly discuss some examples of responsible behavior. (Do chores at home, work at school, obey parents, be honest, help others, and admit if we break a rule rather than blaming others.) If using puppets, select students to represent the characters in the story. After giving out the puppets, explain that when they hear their character (puppet) talk in the story, they are to raise the puppet so the other students can see which animal is talking. Tell the students to listen to the story so they will be able to tell what Lucky Lambkin and Corky Colt learned about taking responsibility for their behavior.

The Gate

School was over and it was Friday night. Since it was in September, the sun was still shining brightly as Lucky Lambkin and Corky Colt were playing ball in Lucky's backyard. Buster, Lucky's new little puppy, was jumping to get the ball as each youngster threw it. "Stop that, Buster," said Lucky.

"Oh, he just likes to play ball, too," said Corky. Then he looked over the fence to see some of their second-grade friends coming down the sidewalk. "Hi, Billy. What are you guys doing?"

"Ted and I are going to the park to play some ball. Do you guys want to come along?" asked Billy Goat as he and Ted Turkey came over to the fence.

"I'll ask mom," said Lucky. He ran into the house, "Mom, Ted and Billy want Corky and me to go play ball at the park. Can we go, please?"

Mrs. Lambkin smiled as she said, "All right. You two can go for an hour, then you must come home because we'll have dinner around 6 p.m."

"Thanks, mom," Lucky said as he turned to run outside.

"Just a minute, Lucky," his mother said, "You have to be sure to feed Buster and lock him in his dog run because he is still a puppy and will try to follow you boys. He can't go with you because he gets distracted and chases squirrels and besides he might get lost."

"Sure, mom," Lucky said as he ran out the door.

"Mom says we can go but we have to be back in about an hour," Lucky told Corky and the four excited boys ran down the sidewalk toward the park.

They had great fun playing ball in the park and even met some new kids who played with them. After the four boys had played ball for a while, they went over to the play area and chased each other through the Jungle Jim maze. Lucky and Ted scared each other on the teeter-totter while Ted and Billy got the merry-go-round going really fast. Finally, after seeing how high they could go on the swings, they raced each other on the monkey bars with Billy beating everyone. Then they all sat down on the grass, all tuckered out and happy.

"Geez, this is fun," said Corky.

"Yeah, I wish we didn't have to go home," said Ted.

"We better hurry," said Lucky. "Corky and I have to be home by six and it must be that time by now."

As they all headed home, Corky and Lucky talked about what a fun time they had and made plans to go to the park again on Saturday.

When they got back to Lucky's house, Lucky took one look at the backyard and said, "Oh, my gosh, I forgot to feed Buster and put him in his dog run and look, the gate is open. We must have left it unlatched. Let's see if Buster stayed in the backyard, 'cause if he didn't, I'm going to be in real trouble."

They looked and Buster was gone. Lucky knew he'd have to go in and tell his mother what he had done.

Mrs. Lambkin was busy cooking dinner when Lucky told her about Buster. She was really angry with Lucky because he did not use responsible behavior and did not feed the dog and put him in his dog run. She told the boys they had to go around the neighborhood and find Buster before dinner. "You need to stay in the neighborhood because I don't want you wandering around the town."

The boys hurried out the door and walked across the street from each other calling for Buster. They had covered about four blocks before they met at the end of the street and Lucky said, "I'm worried that we'll never find him. I sure blew it. I didn't take my responsibility and put him in the dog run. I'm going to feel terrible if Buster gets run over or stolen."

Corky tried to make Lucky feel better, "He'll come back. Let's go around the next two blocks and see if we can find him."

Off they went. Pretty soon, Lucky said, "Stop. Do you hear that barking? I think it's Buster. Come on."

Sure enough, just down the block there was Buster with his two front paws on a tree and barking up at a squirrel on a limb.

Lucky ran up to Buster and put his arms around him and hugged him, "You silly dog, why did you run away?" Then Lucky grabbed Buster's collar and the two boys led him home with Lucky stopping every once in a while to hug Buster.

⚠ Discussion Questions

1. What did Lucky forget to do? (Forgot to feed Buster and put him in the dog run.)

2. Why was that Lucky's responsibility? (His mother asked him to do it before he went to the park.)

3. What happened because Lucky did not practice responsible behavior? (Buster ran away.)

4. What was Lucky's consequence for his lack of responsible behavior? (He and Corky had to go find Buster.)

5. How did Lucky feel when he couldn't find Buster? (Worried)

Second Grade Lesson 1: To Be Responsible

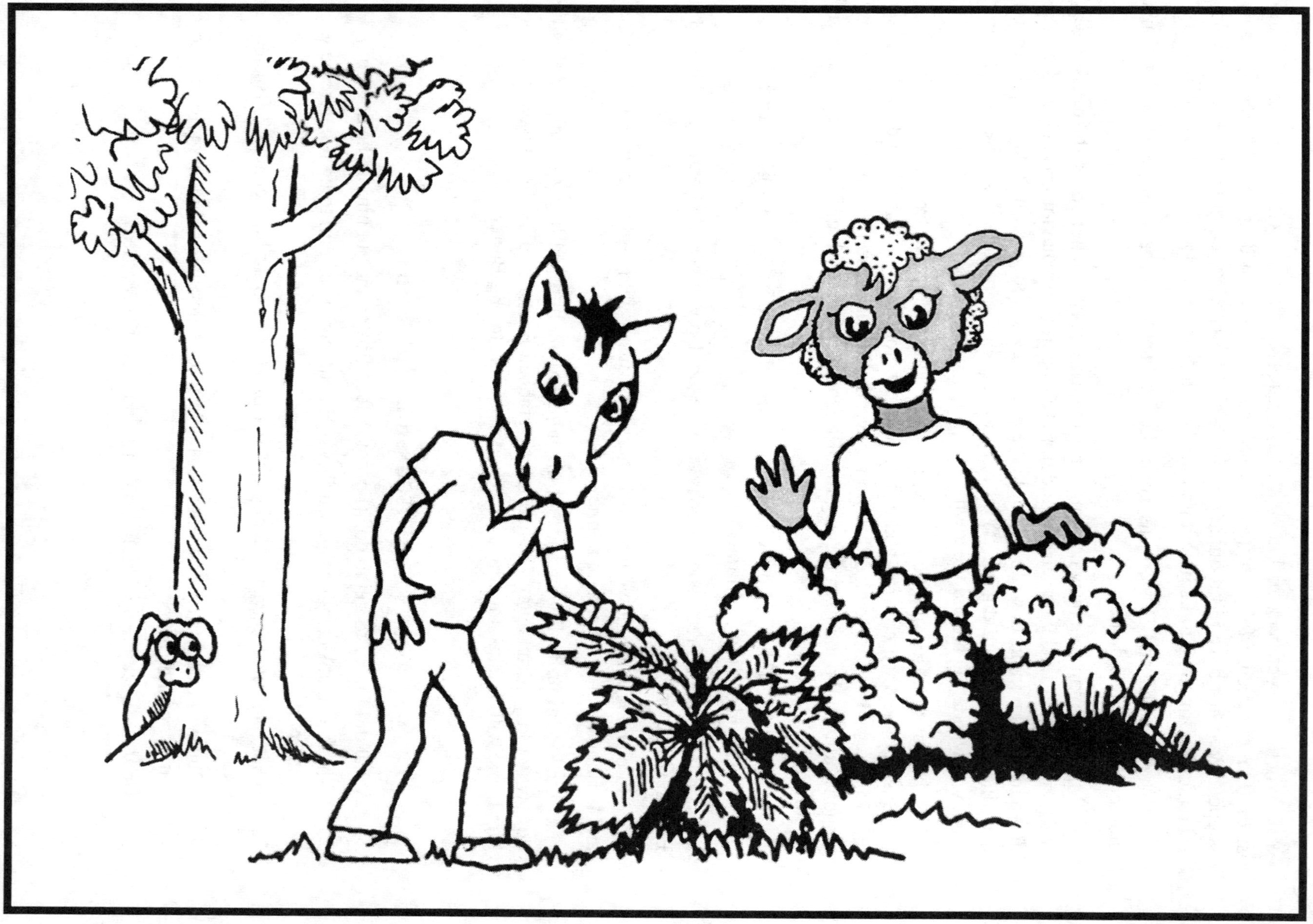

☆ Activities

1. Tell about a time when you forgot to take care of the family pet. What happened?
2. Draw (or paste) a collage of the chores at home that are your responsibility.

☆ Role Play

How would you show responsibility in the following situations . . .

1. This week it is your turn to bring in the playground equipment and Rich wants you to skip it and hurry to line up for gym class.
2. You volunteered to bring cheese to class for a science experiment and Amanda wants to eat it.
3. It is your turn to do dishes and your sister wants you to play.
4. Your mom told you that it is your responsibility to pick up the toys in the living room and you are tired.
5. You forgot to put paper under your art project and Jon bumped your arm and paint spilled on the table.
6. You and Mike are jumping in the kitchen and spill juice all over the floor.
7. You and Darcy were supposed to be at your house at five and she wants to stop at Betsy's house and play.
8. The rule is that you are to ride the bus home from school and Austin wants you to walk home with him.
9. Mom and you are in the car ready to drive to school when you remember that you need your school supplies.
10. Sara, Jordan, and Matt are waiting for you to go out and play so you consider asking Jill to put your food tray away.

☑ Lesson 2
Responsibility Is Important

> Responsibility Is Important — Responsibility is the obligation to be accountable and trustworthy. This is valuable because others respect a person who is dependable and reliable.

Responsibility is important because when we are accountable for our own actions, others will respect us. They know we are responsible because we are dependable. If we take on a job, like feeding the dog then we will do it and if for some reason we can't, we make sure that someone else feeds the dog. If our teacher gives us an assignment, she knows we will do it or try our best. If we tell our friends something we will do, they know we will do it because being responsible is important to us. Being responsible is not always easy because things come up, like playing a game when we know we should be home, but since we know that others depend on us, we take our responsibility seriously. Because we know responsibility is important, we can feel powerful and in charge of our lives when we do our jobs.

Directions: Read and discuss introduction. Ask students what they learned about responsibility in Lesson 1. (To be responsible means to be accountable, dependable, and trustworthy.) Have students name some possible responsibilities of a second grader. (Do chores, work at school, respect others, be honest, be a good listener, and admit if we break a rule or make a mistake.) Tell students that in this lesson we will be looking at some nursery-rhyme characters to see how responsible they are. Listen so you will be able to discuss how important it is to be responsible. The first nursery rhyme is "Little Bo Peep."

Little Bo Peep

Little Bo Peep has lost her sheep
And can't tell where to find them.
Leave them alone
And they'll come home
Wagging their tails behind them.

⚠ Discussion Questions

1. What has Little Bo Peep lost? (Her sheep)
2. What do you think could have happened to them? (Various answers)
3. Who was responsible for taking care of the sheep? (Little Bo Peep)

4. Was Little Bo Peep practicing responsible behavior? (She wouldn't have lost them if she was practicing responsible behavior.)

5. Do you think the sheep will come home wagging their tails behind them? (Probably not since they will go where grass is or various answers.)

(The teacher tells students to listen to "My Little Dog" so they will be able to tell who is responsible and give some reasons why taking responsibility is important.)

My Little Dog

Where, oh, where has my little dog gone?
Where, oh, where can he be?
With his tail cut short and his ears quite long
Where, oh, where is he?

I took him for a walk one day
And we had lots of fun.
I took him off the leash to play
And away he did run.

⚠ Discussion Questions

1. What has been lost? (Little dog)

2. Describe the dog. (He has a short tail and long ears.)

3. Who was responsible for taking care of the little dog? (The owner)

4. Describe how the dog ran away. (The owner took the leash off to let the dog play.)

5. Is finding the little dog important? (Yes, because the person who owns it is upset and the dog could be lost or hurt.)

6. Have you ever lost your pet? Did you find it?

7. Why is it important to be responsible when caring for a pet? (Various answers including possibility that pet could be hurt or even die if its owner did not believe being responsible is important.)

🦎 Activities

1. The teacher asks students to think about the nursery rhyme "Little Boy Blue" and has one student say the poem. Lead students in discussing what was lost and who was responsible.

2. Then if teacher wishes, she may have one student tell the nursery rhyme "The Three Little Kittens" and discuss what was lost and who was responsible for caring for the items.

🧎 Role Play

How would you show responsible behavior in the following situations . . .

1. It's time to feed your dog and Johnny and you are playing ball.

2. You promised your mother you would come straight home from school but your friend wants you to go to their house and play on the computer.

3. Teacher gave you a math assignment as homework and you left it at school.

4. You broke a glass in the kitchen and thought you might clean it up and not tell your mother.

5. You're supposed to walk your little sister home from school but you want to stay and play with your friends so you are considering sending her home with the neighbor girl.

6. You were swinging the bat and you accidentally hit your friend in the head and you are considering saying Tom did it.

7. You promised your friend you would bring a milk jug to school for the science experiment and you forgot.

8. You lost your brother's favorite video and he wants to know where it is.

9. You went to the store with your new friend and you saw him take a candy bar.

10. It's time to clean desks in your room and you're considering taking the things out and just throwing everything back in.

☑ Lesson 3
I Am Special

Special — Everyone is valuable and unique. Being special is knowing that no one else looks like you, no one else talks like you, no one else thinks like you. You are one of a kind.

You know you are special because no one else has the same nose, fingernails, or fingerprints. No one else has the exact same color of hair. No one else has the same shape or color of eyes. No one else talks the same as you do. No one else has the same place in your family. No one else has the same talents and abilities you have. We are all special and valuable and we are each in charge of our own feelings. It is our responsibility to stand up for ourselves and be in charge of our feelings by telling ourselves that we are special and naming one or more of our talents and abilities.

Directions: Read and discuss the introduction then have the students name some examples of responsible behavior (do chores at home, work at school, obey parents, respect others, be a good listener, and admit if we break a rule or make a mistake). Ask what responsibility has to do with being special (it is our responsibility to take care of ourselves and our feelings). Before reading the story, discuss with the students the three things that are important for students to do to handle situations to keep feeling special even when they are being put down: 1. Say: *Stop it, I don't like it. It hurts my feelings.* 2. Tell yourself: *I am special and name one thing that you're good at doing.*

If using puppets for the lesson, select students to represent the characters in the story and have them stand where they can be seen by other students. After giving out the puppets, explain that when they hear their character talk in the story they are to raise the puppet so the other students can see which animal is talking. Tell the students to listen to the story so they will be able to tell what Polly, Cherry, and Lilly learned about being special.

Feeling Special

Second-grade teacher Mrs. Giraffe had a new little girl in class when school started that Monday morning. "Students, I want you to welcome Polly Pigeon. She is new to our school. She came to us from Treasure Elementary School in Rainbow Bridge, Alabama. I want you all to make Polly feel welcome. Polly, do you want to tell us a little about your school?"

"No," Polly said hanging her head and standing on one leg.

"That's all right, Polly," Mrs. Giraffe said with a smile. "Now, you take that desk over there and we'll all stand and say the Pledge of Allegiance."

That morning went well for Polly, except once when she had to answer a question about a story and everybody laughed when she said, "Ah kain't tell you-all what the little chick'n said but ah know she thought th' sky was a'fall'n."

Mrs. Giraffe stopped the story discussion and said, "Students, I am disappointed in your behavior. Remember yesterday when we were discussing how everyone is special and deserves respect. We must each remember that these differences are what makes each of us special and unique."

At recess time, Cherry Chicken was on the merry-go-round when she saw Polly hopping up to get on. "Oh, little baby, you can't get on now."

Lilly Lambkin looked at Cherry and said, "Sometimes you are so funny, Cherry," and they both laughed.

Susie Squirrel kind of squirmed and said, "I think you were mean, Cherry."

"Oh, I didn't mean anything," said Cherry. "Let's go over and make the little chubby baby feel better."

Now, Cherry was one of the most popular girls in second grade and everyone liked being with her because she kept things really exciting and fun. But Susie thought that it was sometimes hard to be on Cherry's side about everything.

Polly had a bad day that Monday and told her mother she really missed her old school and wished she was there but she wouldn't say why.

For the next few days, Cherry seemed to like to show off in front of her friends by saying put-downs to Polly whenever she got a chance. Polly didn't know what to do about it.

Thursday at noon recess, Polly just stood watching the girls play on the jungle gym and leaned against the school wall. Then she saw three of the girls coming over her way.

Cherry, Lilly, and Susie walked over to the side of the building where Polly was standing on one leg again. Susie said, "Polly, do you want to play?"

Polly shyly said, "Yes, ah really do."

Susie and Polly ran to the swings and got two swings side by side.

"You have to stand up to Cherry," Susie said as they were swinging. "When she starts calling you names tell her, 'Stop it, I don't like it. That hurts my feelings.' "

"Won't that make Cherry angry with me?" Polly asked.

"No," said Susie. "Cherry will respect you if you stand up to her. Mrs. Giraffe said that when we are being put down, it is important to know how to stand up for ourselves."

"What are we supposed to do?" asked Polly.

"Let's see if I can remember," Susie said. "1. Say: *Stop it, I don't like it. It hurts my feelings.* 2. Tell myself: *I am special and name one thing that I am good at doing.* There, I remembered it." "What are you good at?"

"Well, ah love t' dance and ah'm good at dancin'," said Polly with a smile.

Just then Cherry and Lilly came up to the girls and took the next two swings.

Cherry said, "Well, little friends, what's going on over here? Poor little Polly, are you complaining because you want to be at your own school? Well, face it, little bird, you're here and you better get used to it."

With a sigh and look at Susie, Polly got off the swing and stood up straight. "Stop it. Ah don't like it. It hurts ma feelings when you put me down. Ah'm special," said Polly. Then she said to herself, "Ah'm special an' ah'm a good dancer."

As Polly walked away, Cherry got off her swing and said, "Really, what on earth did I say that got her feathers up?"

"You know what you've been doing," said Susie as she ran after Polly.

Lilly looked a bit embarrassed as she said, "Cherry, we both have been putting Polly down. It just seemed like fun but it hurt her feelings."

"Yeh, I guess you're right," Cherry said as she hung her head. "I really didn't mean to hurt her feelings. I was just teasing her."

"Come on, Cherry," Lilly said. "You were really trying to get to her. And the sad thing is, I thought it was funny."

"It wasn't really funny, was it?" said Cherry. "I don't know why I was doing it. I guess I was showing off for you guys and it was so easy to get Polly upset, but that's no excuse, is it?"

"No, it isn't," Lilly agreed. "We have to do something to make up for what we did."

"First thing," said Cherry, "is apologize to Polly."

Meanwhile, Susie was telling Polly how well she did. "You really stuck up for yourself with Cherry. See, I told you it would work. Cherry is really nice but sometimes she likes to show off."

Just then, Cherry and Lilly came up to Susie and Polly.

"Polly, I apologize for being so mean to you this week," said Cherry. "I just forgot what Mrs. Pigeon has been telling us and I'm sorry. I am special and so are you. Thank you for reminding me."

"And, I'm sorry I was joining Cherry," said Lilly. "I hope you can forgive us because this Saturday I'm going to have some of my friends come over and play games in my backyard. Do you want to come?"

11

"That sounds like fun," said Cherry. "We really want to get to know you better."

"Ah'd really like to, but Ah have to ask ma mum tonight. Would it be al'right if ah tell you tomorrow?" asked Polly.

⚠ Discussion Questions

1. Who was the new student? (Polly Pigeon)

2. Who put Polly down? (Cherry Chicken)

3. How did Polly feel? (Hurt)

4. What did Cherry do to put her down? (Called her names, made fun of her, and wouldn't play with her.)

5. Why do you think Cherry put Polly down? (Various answers like, she was showing off, she doesn't feel good about herself, she's had put-downs said to her before.)

6. What did Lilly do? (Went along with Cherry)

7. What did Susie do? (She made friends with Polly and helped her.)

8. How did Susie help Polly? (She told her how to stand up for herself. 1. Say: *Stop it, I don't like it. It hurts my feelings.* 2. Tell yourself: *I am special and tell yourself one thing you're good at doing.*)

9. Was Polly able to feel special again? (Yes) How? (She did the things Susie taught her to do.)

10. What lesson did Cherry and Lilly learn? (Learned everyone is special and deserves respect.)

🐝 Activities

1. Teach students the "I Am Special" song (see Appendix B, Resource Sheet 1). Have them sing it several times.

2. Have students write about a time when they were put down. Have each student share it with the class and tell what they would do next time using the two steps.

3. Have students draw a picture of something they are good at and tell about it to the class.

🏃 Role Play

Guide the role play so the students will practice the two steps to standing up for themselves and keeping their special feeling.

How would you handle the situation, if . . .

1. Every time that Johnny sees you, he calls you a "nerd."
2. Bill won't let you play ball because he says you play like a sissy.
3. Your big sister tells you you are stupid.
4. Betsy makes fun of your clothes.
5. Jill tells you you can't play at her house.
6. Molly told you to skip the dessert at lunch so you won't get bigger.
7. The kid that sits behind you always pulls your hair.
8. You have an accent (talk differently) and people make fun of you.
9. You go out to recess and your best friend, Donna, ignores you.
10. You make mistakes reading out loud in class and Mark tells you you should go back to first grade.

☑ Lesson 4
Cooperation

> Cooperation — Cooperation is the act of working together; united effort.

Some things are easier to do with more than one person so sometimes we all have to work together to get a task done. This is called cooperation. Sometimes teachers want us to cooperate on projects because they think we need to practice our responsibility as a part of a team and work together with others. Cooperation isn't always easy because sometimes we think we know the answer and we want to be the one to get the credit. Sometimes we have to remember that everybody on the team or in the group has a right to express their opinion and help with the project or play in the game. When we take the responsibility to cooperate with others, we often find out that others have different ideas and sometimes they are very good ideas. We would never know this if we didn't cooperate, listen, and learn.

Directions: Read and discuss introduction. Review examples of responsible behavior. (Do chores at home, work at school, obey parents, be honest, help others, take charge of our feelings, admit if we break a rule, rather than blaming others.) Discuss why it takes responsibility to cooperate and work in a group or on a team. If using puppets, select students to represent characters in the story. After giving out the puppets, explain that when they hear their character (puppet) talk in the story, they are to raise the puppet so the other students can see which animal is talking. Then tell students you are going to read a story about second graders who will be working on a science project and tell them to listen carefully to see what happened because one of the characters did not cooperate.

The County Fair

The students in Mr. Moose's class were excited. Today was the day they got into their groups to plan their county-fair project. Mr. Moose had chosen the groups yesterday and Lucky Lambkin was happy because one of his friends, Corky Colt, was in his group. Also in Lucky's group were Susie Squirrel and Kathy Kat.

Before Mr. Moose had the youngsters get into their groups the class brainstormed ideas for group projects and listed several ideas on the board for the students to pick from. Some named were a blacksmith shop, an early-American kitchen, an Indian village, a medieval castle, an earth and moon, and the sun and planets. Other possible projects were writing a history of Anytown, USA, drawing an Anytown street map and a map of the city park.

The members of Lucky's group decided that they wanted to do one of the projects where they could build something. The two girls wanted to do the early-American kitchen, but Lucky and Corky vetoed that. They wanted to do a blacksmith shop but the girls said no. Lucky said, "Okay, then let's see if we can find one we all want to build."

"I guess an Indian village would be fun," suggested Susie. "We could make a stream and have some Indians washing clothes or fishing."

"Sounds great," Lucky said. "I think it would be fun to make a campfire and tepee. What do you think, Corky?"

"Yeh, I like it, too," said Corky.

"Me, too," said Kathy. "We all have to decide what we want to do. Susie and I could make the Indian women with a little child out of clay and put them near the stream. I have some clay at home that I will bring tomorrow."

"Okay," said Lucky. "Corky and I will make the tepee and fire. I've got some leather at home that we could use for the tepee."

"Hey," exclaimed Corky. "I have a great piece of leather that I want to bring for the tepee. I want to be in charge of making the tepee."

"That's all right with me," said Lucky. "I'll do the campfire. I can use some little sticks that look like logs and put them inside some pebbles. I have some red plastic paper at home that will look just like fire."

"Let's just light the sticks," said Corky who is always ready for excitement.

"Don't be silly, Corky. That would be dangerous," said Kathy.

"Aw, you never have any fun," grumbled Corky .

"Everybody remember to bring your supplies tomorrow because Mr. Moose said we have to be ready to start our projects next Monday," said Susie. "You know we have to enter our project in the county fair next Thursday."

"Sure . . . sure . . . Miss Know-it-all," said Corky .

The next day, Friday, everyone cooperated and brought their supplies except Corky.

"Corky," Susie reminded him at recess, "remember the stuff for the tepee Monday because that's when we start working on our project."

"Sure, I'll remember," Corky said as he went off to play ball.

Monday morning after recess, the groups got back together and started work on their projects. Mr. Moose told them they would be working on the projects every day until Thursday when they would take a trip to the county-fair building so they could set up their projects.

Corky had forgotten his tepee sticks and leather so the group decided they needed some animals, but when Corky started to make them out of clay, he just rolled it into little balls and played marbles. The girls just kept working on two Indian women and a little baby. Lucky was busy setting up his campfire and he put his pebbles in a circle and set the sticks inside.

Corky took his clay and wandered over to Billy Goat's group and started giving Billy's group suggestions on how to make their castle. Billy told him to butt out so Corky wandered from group to group until Mr. Moose said, "Corky, this is a cooperative group activity and you should be working with your group."

Corky mumbled something and went back to his group.

The next two days, Corky continued to be uncooperative by forgetting his leather and wandering around bothering the other groups instead of even helping make animals for the Indian village.

"Corky," said Lucky. "You only have tomorrow to get the leather here and build the tepee."

"Aw, don't worry," said Corky. "I always come through."

Lucky did worry, though, and when Corky was wandering around the room Wednesday, he told the girls he was making a tepee at home with his leather and he would bring it Thursday just in case Corky didn't. "And if he does, we can have two tepees," said Lucky.

Sure enough, Corky didn't bring his leather Thursday but Lucky brought his finished tepee.

Susie and Kathy had finished the clay figures and put little scraps of material on them that looked like Indian dresses, even with fringe. They even had some extra clothes to lay on the beach and had one of the women bending over washing clothes in the stream, made of blue paper with a rocky beach that Lucky had helped them make.

When Lucky put his tepee up, the girls smiled and said it looked great with the pictures Lucky had drawn on the leather with felt markers.

Corky said, "I could have made a terrific tepee if I would have remembered my leather." When it was time to take the projects to the fair building, Corky felt kind of bad that he had let his group down. Mr. Moose looked at him and said, "You haven't cooperated with your group much, have you? Do you really think your name should be listed on the project card?"

"I guess not," said Corky, hanging his head. "Does that mean I can't go to the fair to help set the project up?"

Mr. Moose said, "Yes, you can go but your group must decide if you deserve to help them set up the project and whether or not you deserve to have your name listed on the project card."

At the fair building, Corky said to his group, "I'd like to help you put the project up but I don't think I should have my name on the card because I really didn't cooperate with you guys and do my part. I'm really sorry I blew it but I've learned my lesson. I know how bad I will feel when my parents come to the fair and don't see my name on any project. If you ever let me be in a group with you again, I know it is my responsibility to be cooperative and work with the group."

Lucky said, "Okay, sounds fair that you don't put your name on the project card but you can help us set up the village."

"Hey, guys," said Susie. "Let's get busy."

⚠ Discussion Questions

1. Who was in the group in the story? (Lucky, Corky, Susie, and Kathy)
2. Which project did Lucky's group choose? (Indian village)
3. Did every member of the group cooperate and help on the project? (No, Corky didn't.)
4. What was Corky doing instead of helping with the project? (Forgetting his leather for the tepee, wandering around disturbing others, and playing marbles with the clay)
5. What did Corky learn about cooperation? (It is your responsibility to cooperate with your group and do your job.)
6. What happened because Corky didn't take responsibility for his part of the project? (He didn't get to have his name on the project.)
7. How did Corky feel when he realized how badly he had let his group down? (Sad)
8. Tell about a time you did not cooperate. What happened?
9. Tell about a time when someone in your group did not cooperate.

𝕏 Activities

1. Draw a picture of Corky showing how he felt at the end of the story.
2. In groups, have students make some of the projects suggested in the story. Ask students to pay attention to how everyone cooperates.

Role Play

How would you cooperate in the following situations . . .

1. Your mom asked your brother and you to do the dishes.

2. You are working on a science project with George.

3. You're getting ready to play kick ball and Ben knows different rules.

4. Your teacher asked Debbie and you to clean out the book shelf.

5. Jill, Jon, Bob, and you are going to jump rope.

6. Your sister and you want to use the computer at the same time.

7. Your brother and you are setting up a board game and your brother is grabbing everything.

8. You don't like the new outfit your mother wants you to wear to school.

9. You are babysitting your little sister and she wants a cookie but she is not allowed to have one.

10. Jim, Don, and you are working on math together.

☑ Lesson 5
Kindness

> Kindness — Kindness is the ability to do good, be gentle, tenderhearted and forgiving, and to help each other.

Being kind is thinking about and considering the feelings of others. Sometimes it helps to think how you would feel if someone were unkind to you and did things that hurt your feelings. Kindness has a lot to do with caring and showing it. Some of the people we care about that we can show kindness to are our family, friends, and neighbors. Kindness is treating others like we want to be treated. It is everyone's responsibility to behave in a kind manner to all others and take responsibility for our behavior when we don't.

Directions: Read and discuss introduction. Review examples of responsible behavior such as do our homework, take care of our feelings, obey parents, cooperate with others, and do chores at home. Ask students how they think responsibility relates to kindness. (It is our responsibility to treat others with kindness and respect.) If using puppets, have students lift the puppets when they hear their character's name in the following story. Tell students to listen to the story so they will be able to understand how important it is to treat others with kindness.

The Cinderella Watch

At noon recess Lilly Lambkin, Cherry Chicken, and Ted Turkey ran outside to jump rope. Right behind them came Susie Squirrel, Polly Pigeon, and Corky Colt. Doolee Dog and Kathy Kat came running also.

"I got two long jump ropes from the teacher," said Polly. "Let's all jump rope then trade places while we keep the ropes going."

"Sounds like fun," said Lilly. "You guys start. I want to see if Billy Goat wants to play jump rope with us. I'll be right back."

The second graders got ready with Cherry and Ted turning the rope for Susie and Corky. Kathy and Polly started turning the rope for Doolee. In a minute, Lilly was back and jumped right in with Doolee without missing a beat. They thought it was neat that they were jumping in rhythm with the other group.

"Whee, this is fun!" panted Corky as the turners stepped up the pace, going faster and faster.

"The first one to miss has to turn the jump rope," said Cherry.

It was a fun time and with two jump ropes going everybody got several turns to jump.

When recess was over, they all headed back to the class room, laughing and agreeing to do it again that afternoon. Suddenly Lilly stopped.

She yelled, "Oh no! I lost my Cinderella watch!" She wanted to go right back and look for it but Polly said, "We have to go in or we will be late. Tell the teacher and maybe she will let us go back out and hunt for it."

On the way into the room Lilly asked Mrs. Giraffe if she could go back outside and look for the watch.

"I'll send Miss Sparrow, the teacher assistant, out to help you hunt," Mrs. Giraffe said.

Miss Sparrow took Lilly's hand and said, "Where were you playing?"

Lilly took Miss Sparrow to where they were jumping rope and both of them looked all around for about 15 minutes. Then Miss Sparrow said, "I'm sorry, Lilly, but it just isn't here and we must go in now. I'll help you look again at recess time, honey. Maybe we can find it then."

At afternoon recess, not only did Miss Sparrow help look for the watch but so did all the rest of the rope jumpers. No luck. Everyone sympathized with Lilly because they knew the watch was important to her. Ever since she had learned to tell time, she had worn it practically every day.

Lilly was pretty sad for the rest of the day. After school she wanted to stay and look again but Lucky said, "Mom is picking us up to take us to T-ball practice so we don't have time. I'll help you look for it in the morning."

Mrs. Lambkin wasn't angry about the watch. She said, "I'm sorry you lost your watch. I know you're probably feeling bad about it because I know it was special to you."

After T-ball practice, Lilly was still feeling bad but remembered that she could look again the next day.

The next morning at recess, the friends were out looking again. It had just disappeared. In fact, they had no luck all day even when Lilly remembered she had gone to the ball field to ask Billy if he wanted to play.

By the end of the day Lilly was beginning to realize she wouldn't ever find her Cinderella watch.

That night at home, Cherry told her mother about Lilly losing her Cinderella watch. "Gee, mom," Cherry said, "Lilly loved that watch. I have a Cinderella watch that I never wear because I like my Sleeping Beauty watch better. Do you think it would be all right if I gave Lilly my watch?"

"Why, honey," said Mrs. Chicken, "I think that would be so kind and generous of you. It shows you are a caring person."

So the next day, Cherry could hardly wait to see Lilly and in class couldn't resist whispering to her that she had a surprise for her. On the way out to recess, Cherry said, "Lilly, I know we couldn't find your Cinderella watch yesterday, but I have something for you." And she handed Lilly her Cinderella watch.

"Oh, Cherry," Lilly said. "That's your watch. You can't give it to me."

"Yes, I can. My mom even said it was all right," said Cherry smiling. "Besides, I really like my Sleeping Beauty watch and I don't need two watches."

"Oh, I just love it. What a kind thing to do. You are a wonderful friend," exclaimed Lilly as she hugged Cherry and fastened her watch on her arm. "This one is even more special than the one I lost because a friend gave it to me." And off Lilly and Cherry went to show Lilly's watch to everyone.

⚠ Discussion Questions

1. What did Lilly lose? (Cinderella watch)

2. Did she find it? (No)

3. What did Lilly's friends do? (They helped her try to find it.)

4. How did Lilly feel about losing the watch? (She felt sad.)

5. What did Cherry decide to do? (Give Lilly her Cinderella watch.)

6. What do you think of Cherry's decision?

7. Tell about a time when you showed kindness. How did you feel?

8. Tell about a time when someone was kind to you. How did you feel?

🏃 Activities

1. Divide your paper into four parts. On each part, draw a picture of a time when you were kind to someone or they were kind to you.

2. Think of a kind act you can do before the end of the day and do it. Be prepared to discuss it tomorrow. (Suggestions: Help a friend with school work, hold a door open, loan a pencil, help the teacher, invite someone to play, help your brother or sister do chores, help your mother or father.)

𝕏 Role Play

How would you show kindness if . . .

1. Sue drops her books in the hall.
2. Your brother is in a hurry to go to soccer practice, but has to do the dishes first.
3. Your scout leader is handing out art supplies.
4. The new student is looking for his classroom.
5. Jon needs a drink but you're in line in front of him.
6. Betsy is having trouble understanding triple-digit subtraction.
7. At recess, Dory is sitting on the steps looking sad and left out.
8. The house is a mess and mom is expecting company.
9. When playing baseball, Pam is having trouble hitting the ball.
10. Your sister broke her favorite toy.

☑ Lesson 6
Honesty

Honesty – Honesty is when you tell the truth.

Being honest at all times is very important if we want to have the trust and respect of others. Even if we make a mistake and are scared to admit it, others will be proud of us for telling the truth. If we have a habit of lying about things and people find out we lie, then they will not believe us. When we hear the saying "honesty is the best policy," it is essential that we know that this is important.

Directions: Read and discuss introduction. Ask students what they have been learning about responsible behavior this year and name some second-graders' responsibilities. (Do chores, take charge of our feelings, cooperate with others, be kind, and take responsibility for our behavior.) Ask what students think responsibility has to do with honesty. (It is always our responsibility to be honest and tell the truth.) After giving out the puppets, explain that when the students hear their character (puppet) talk in the story, they are to raise the puppet so the other students can see which animal is talking. Tell the students to listen carefully to the story today so they will be able to tell what the Sunshine Elementary School students learn about honesty.

Pinocchio

Summer was over and all the students were excited about going back to school at Sunshine Elementary. They were happily chatting about their summer vacations and the report they were going to give in Mr. Moose's class right after recess.

Kathy Kat told about going to Canada and riding on the ferry to Vancouver Island where she got to visit the wax museum and the famous Victorian gardens. She thought all the wax statues looked real, especially the one of Elvis Presley.

Susie Squirrel said she was thrilled when she and her family took the mules all the way down to the bottom of the Grand Canyon. "It was really, really deep!" she exclaimed.

"I went to Nashville and I got to see the Dixie Chicks sing and I was so excited," exclaimed Minnie Moo who likes to pretend she is a singing cowgirl. "When I grow up, I'm going to go there and become a famous singer."

"I went to the best place," said Billy Goat. "I went to the statue of Liberty and got to climb way up high and look out over the water. It was great! "

23

Just then Polly Pigeon came up and asked what they were talking about. Billy told her that Mr. Moose had asked all the second graders in his class to give an oral report on their vacations.

"Gee," said Polly. "I hope Mrs. Giraffe asks us to talk about our vacations, too. I had great fun going on a rafting trip on the Snake River at Lewiston, Idaho and we got to ride on rubber rafts through lots of white water. It was fun and scary."

Corky Colt said he was going to give his report about his great time at Knox Berry Farm and Disney Land in California. "It was so much fun riding all the rides. I liked Space Mountain best." Then he turned to Lucky Lambkin and asked, "What are you going to do your report on?"

Lucky hesitated before he said, "Um, Disney World in Florida . . . that's where we went. I got to see Mickey Mouse and Donald Duck and got to ride on the most exciting rides."

Just then the bell rang and Lucky looked around, "I'll tell you all more about it when I give the report. We have to go in now."

At noon recess, the students were again talking about the reports they had just given.

"Everyone did such exciting things," said Corky. "Didn't they, Lucky?"

"Yeah," said Lucky. "Let's go play ball now."

Just then Lilly Lambkin, Lucky's twin sister, came up and Billy asked her, "What was your favorite ride at Disney World?"

"Where?" said Lilly. "I've never been to Disney World. We didn't get a vacation this year because dad had to work."

All the students from Mr. Moose's room who were standing around looked at Lucky.

"Wow, Lucky," said Corky. "If you keep lying like that, you're going to have a nose like Pinocchio. You remember the story Mr. Moose read us about how the more Pinocchio lied, the longer his nose got. Hey, everybody, check out Lucky's nose. Does it look like Pinocchio's?"

Kathy said, "Lucky, you were wrong to lie. None of us will trust you if you are not honest. You even wrote a report on your Disney World vacation."

Lucky hung his little woolly head.

Lilly looked at her brother with sympathy for she knew how much both of them had wanted to go on a fun vacation, but she couldn't understand why he would lie about it. "Lucky, you were not honest. You have to tell Mr. Moose the truth."

"Yeah, I guess I'd better go in now and tell him," Lucky said sadly.

As the other students ran off to play ball, Lilly walked with Lucky to the door of his room and said, "Good luck, Lucky."

Lucky went inside and Mr. Moose looked up from his desk, "Why, hello, Lucky. What brings you back in before recess is over?"

Lucky stood hanging his head for a moment, then took a deep breath and said, "Mr. Moose, I lied. We didn't go to Disney World this summer. We didn't get to go anywhere. I'm sorry but I wanted to have someplace special to talk about, too. Will my nose grow long like Pinocchio's?"

Mr. Moose said seriously, "No, Lucky, your nose won't grow but lying is a serious thing."

Lucky said, "Can I stay in for the rest of the recess and erase the boards for you. I'm embarrassed to go back outside with my friends. They are never going to trust me again."

Mr. Moose said, "You're right. You'll have to earn back their trust. But, I guess it's all right if you stay in the rest of this recess. Just remember, you must face them at the afternoon recess. That's part of the consequence of not being honest."

Lucky got busy erasing the board and thought to himself, "Lying isn't worth it. I will always tell the truth after this."

⚠ Discussion Questions

1. What did Lucky lie about? (His vacation)

2. Why did Lucky lie? (He wanted something exciting to talk about.)

3. Even though Lucky thought he had a good reason to lie, did that make it okay? (No, we must always be honest.)

4. How did the students find out Lucky lied? (Lilly told them at recess.)

5. What did Lucky do to make amends for his lie? (He told Mr. Moose he had lied.)

6. What were Lucky's consequences for not being honest? (He was embarrassed to see his friends.)

7. Tell about a time a friend lied to you. What happened?

8. Tell about a time you lied. What happened?

🏃 Activities

1. Have students watch the Pinocchio video or read the story to the students. Have them discuss what happened when Pinocchio lied?

2. Draw a picture of why it is always your responsibility to be honest.

Role Play

How would you practice honesty, if . . .

1. You broke your mother's favorite cup.

2. You copied your spelling test off of Susie's paper.

3. You moved John's checkers when he went to get a drink of water.

4. Mom told you to take 50 cents from her purse and you are thinking of taking a dollar.

5. Dad asked you to water the lawn and you told him you couldn't find the hose.

6. Pam loaned you a marker and you told her you put it back in her desk but you took it home.

7. In kick ball, you knew you were out on first base but you want to tell them you were safe.

8. Jim wanted you to help him steal a toy at the store.

9. You accidentally turned off your dad's program on the computer and lost it and consider telling him your brother did it.

10. Sara left her candy bar on the table and you ate it so you think about telling her you didn't see it.

☑ Lesson 7
Respect

Respect — Respect is when consideration is shown for others, their ideas, their feelings, and their property.

It's important to be considerate and pay attention to others and honor their feelings and ideas as well as their property. This shows that we understand that each of us is worthy of respect because each of us is special and deserves proper consideration. We need to treat others as we would like to be treated. Respect really implies properly honoring the worth of someone or something. When we meet someone we show respect by learning their names and treating them nicely. We might ask them to play with us or find out about them. We also need to show respect to older and wiser people by listening to what they have to say and learning from it. For example, teachers and parents have information to teach us and we show respect by paying attention. Respect also means we show consideration for others' property by taking care of it and treating it gently so that we don't break it.

Directions: Briefly discuss some examples of responsible behavior such as doing chores, helping mother carry groceries in, etc. Discuss the meaning of respect (see above) then have the students tell what they think responsibility has to do with respect. (It is our responsibility to respect others, their ideas, feelings, and property and expect that they will respect us, our ideas, feelings, and property in return.) Tell students to listen to the following story "The Lion and The Mouse" so they can discuss how the two animals showed respect for each other.

The Lion and the Mouse

Lion napped, hidden in tall, golden grass after a busy day of hunting. As Lion slept, a small gray mouse scampered across his face. Lion felt nothing until Mouse's scrawny feet dashed over his nose.

"Ah choo!" sneezed Lion, scratching his nose and capturing Mouse in the same instant.

Lion looked closely at his tiny catch and was about to pop him into his mouth like a peanut when he heard Mouse scream.

"Please let me go," begged Mouse. "You won't regret it. I'll be sure to repay your kindness."

"How silly!" laughed Lion. "Whatever could a tiny fellow like you ever do to help a magnificent creature like me?"

"You never know when a small friend might do great things," pleaded Mouse.

Lion had his doubts. But he kind of liked the mouse and wanted to show some respect for the mouse's opinion. Besides he was tired and began once more to think of finishing his nap. So, in the end, he simply let Mouse go free.

(Option: Teacher may stop here and discuss the following questions.)

1. How did Lion treat Mouse with respect? (Lion listened to Mouse and then let him go.)

2. How did Mouse talk Lion into letting him go? (Mouse said he might be able to repay Lion someday.)

3. Do you think Mouse will ever get to repay Lion his respect? (Various answers)

(Tell the students: Let's continue reading the story to see what happens.)

The very next day, Lion was snared by the thick ropes of a hunter's trap and couldn't get loose. He was worried the hunters would soon be back and he kept trying to get free. While struggling with the cruel ropes around him, Lion was surprised to see Mouse scamper out of the forest.

"I've returned to repay your favor," said Mouse simply.

Then, bit by bit, Mouse chewed and gnawed the rope until finally it snapped and Lion was free from the trap.

As Lion waved goodbye to Mouse, he had one thing to say: "A small friend may become a great friend."

⚠ Discussion Questions

1. How did Mouse show respect for Lion? (He saved his life.)

2. How did Mouse save Lion? (He chewed the rope to set him free before a hunter could kill him.)

3. Because Lion was bigger, did he deserve more respect than Mouse? (No) Why? (Each is a valuable and worthwhile creature and deserves equal respect.)

4. Tell about a time when someone did not respect you.

5. Tell about a time when you did not show respect for another person.

Activities

1. Draw a picture of a time when you showed respect to a person or their property. (Suggestions: A group listens to everyone's ideas for a math project, a classmate suggests a new game to play at recess, an elderly person needs help picking up a book, your friend's coat was laying in the dirt.)

2. Have students share pictures with class.

Role Play

How would you show respect if . . .

1. Johnny wants you to listen to gossip about your friend, Kayla.

2. A classmate's drawing fell off the bulletin board and students in the class were about to step on it.

3. Jill and you are playing on the computer and your mother asks you to rake the yard.

4. You are talking with a friend on the phone when your father tells you he has to use the phone.

5. Tammy said something that seemed silly to you and you wanted to laugh at her.

6. Bob told you that he thought he saw an alien last night and you didn't believe him.

7. Billy threatens to break your favorite pencil box. (Note: Point out that self-respect is important.)

8. The teacher is reading a story and Ann is trying to talk to you.

9. Mom tells your brother and you to do the dishes and you want to ignore her.

10. Tom and you borrowed Bob's fire engine and he told you to be careful because the ladder was ready to break.

☑ Lesson 8
Self-Control

Self-control – Self-control is to have power over or be able to discipline our thoughts, feelings, or behavior. To use self-control we must stop and think before we act.

Having self-control is to be in charge of our behavior. Even if something exciting and fun comes up, we must stop and think before we act. We need to think about the possible consequences of our behavior and use self-control to avoid hurting others. We must ask the question, "What will be the consequences of my behavior?" We must control our actions so that we finish a task that is our responsibility. We also must use self-control in other ways. If we get angry and want to hit someone, we must use self-control. If somebody has something we want, we must use self-control and not grab it. If we see some money laying around, we must use self-control and not just take it but ask whose it is. It is the responsibility of each of us to practice self-control so that we grow up to be someone who can be trusted.

Directions: Read and discuss the introduction. Review some examples of responsible behavior. (Do chores, do homework, be honest, treat others with respect, take charge of our feelings, cooperate, and take responsibility for our behavior rather than blame others.) Ask what responsibility has to do with self-control. (It is our responsibility to stop and think before we act. See above for examples.) Tell the students to listen to the story so they will be able to tell what Corky Colt learned about practicing self-control.

The Unicorn

It was spring break at Sunshine School in Anytown, USA, and Corky Colt was going to visit his great grandmother, whom he had never met. He was so excited about meeting great grandmother, Marvel Mare, that he could hardly sit still on the long drive to Arizona.

The next day when Corky and his parents arrived at Grandmother Marvel's farm, she was waiting for them with open arms. After lunch, Corky was still all charged up from the trip and raring to go; so to burn off some of his energy, Grandmother Marvel sent him out to explore. Corky was really interested in everything around the farm. He looked over the pig pens, the chicken coops, the granary, the pastures, and the barn.

Then he spotted a beautiful buckskin filly grazing in a field just below the barn. He ran over to the fence to talk to this young horse to see if he could pet her. Once there though, he saw that the filly's legs were hobbled with metal braces that kept her from being able to run and jump. Corky, without thinking, opened the gate and quickly went over to the filly and removed the hobbles, saying, "Wow, I'll get rid of these. They must be uncomfortable."

The filly never even whinnied, but immediately reared up and bolted out the gate at full speed. She ripped past Corky so fast that he stood dazed, watching the filly gallop toward the nearby hills.

Corky began to realize the trouble he had caused by not thinking before he acted. He was scared and a sense of dread washed over him as he ran to the barn to tell the stable hand about the missing filly. The ranch hand immediately became extremely distressed and started yelling, "Oh, no! The filly was hobbled to keep her from using her injured leg until it healed and she didn't like that at all. Her running like that could really damage the muscles in that leg."

When Grandmother Marvel heard what had happened, she called Corky into her room to talk. "Corky," she said, "I am very disappointed in your behavior and your lack of self-control. I have sent the hired hand out to find the filly and bring her back and I can only hope that she is all right. Come over here and sit down, Corky. I want to tell you a true story about a time when another young animal didn't use self-control and something terrible happened that changed his life forever." Here is the story she told Corky.

Long ago, there was a family of unicorns who lived in a wonderful, mystical place called Fairyland. It was a cheery place that was covered with beautiful flowers, tall green trees, splendid waterfalls, and colorful rainbows. For centuries the unicorns spent their days running through the beautiful, warm meadows and playing with all of their mystical friends like the gazelle, Pegasus, and the other winged horses. It was a privilege to be able to live in such a place and the unicorns and their friends had been extremely carefree until a group of evil elves came to live in Fairyland. They moved to the other side of the mountain where there was not much light so the land there was cold and dark.

The happy side of Fairyland where the Unicorns lived had a special light source that came from a magic sun tower. The evil elves were quite envious of all the beauty that was created by this powerful tower and they wanted to steal it. All of the mystical animals realized that their carefree days were over and that they must take responsibility to protect the magic tower. It was decided that everyone in the kingdom must participate in helping guard the tower.

There was a young unicorn named Uni and he had a magnificent gold horn that gave him a tremendous sense of pride. Uni's favorite activity was to climb up to the top of a rainbow and slide down the other side. He and his gazelle friends had the most fun sliding down the bumpy side where they bounced up and down so fast that their tummies tickled, causing them to giggle and squeal as they slid faster and faster down the rainbow.

One especially warm, sunny day, Uni was on duty guarding the magic sun tower, when all the young gazelles galloped by, saying they were on their way to play on a rainbow and they were sorry Uni couldn't come along. But, without even looking back, using any self-control, or thinking about the consequences, Uni raced off with his friends to play on the rainbow.

While Uni was off having fun, something terrible happened. The evil elves came and stole the magic sun tower. Everyone in the land immediately knew what happened, because it was mid-afternoon and it quickly became totally dark. The water, trees, grass, and rainbow immediately dried up and turned brown.

The mystical animals were furious with Uni because of his lack of responsible behavior. In fact, everyone was so angry with Uni that his lovely golden horn was taken away and he was banished from Fairyland forever.

Grandmother Marvel went on, "I know this story is true because Uni was the great, great, grandfather of today's horses and this is how his lack of self-control changed their lives. Horses no longer got to live in the magical Fairyland as unicorns but they had to move to the real world and be changed forever."

"Wow, grandmother," said Corky, "I'm glad you told me that story so I can see now how important it is that we all use self-control to keep from causing terrible things to happen. I promise from now on, I will stop and think before I act and if we find the filly, I will feed and care for her for the rest of my visit."

Just then, Ben, the stable hand, reported that the young filly had been caught and was in the stall in the barn.

"Was she all right?" asked Corky.

"We're not sure yet, but her leg looks okay," reported Ben.

Corky looked at his grandmother and said, "I hope my lack of self-control did not hurt that lovely buckskin filly. I also wish Uni would have kept his horn so there would still be unicorns."

⚠ Discussion Questions

1. Where did Corky go? (To grandmother Marvel's farm)
2. How did Corky lose self-control? (He unhooked the filly's leg hobbles.)
3. Who told Corky the Unicorn story? (Grandmother Marvel)
4. Who was Uni? (The great, great grandfather of today's horses.)
5. What did Uni do that showed he lacked self-control? (He left the sun tower to go play.)

6. How did Uni's behavior affect the happy side of Fairyland? (The evil elves stole the sun tower and the land went dark.)

7. What happened to Uni? (He lost his horn and was kicked out of Fairyland.)

8. How was Corky and Uni's behavior similar? (Neither one used self-control so it caused trouble for others around them.)

Activities

1. Draw and color a picture of a time when you either did or didn't use self-control.

2. Share your drawing with the class. If your drawing shows you used self-control, tell how you were able to be responsible. If your drawing shows you did not use self-control, tell about the problems and how you would be more responsible next time.

Role Play

Tell how you would practice self-control if . . .

1. Chelsie and you want to eat the cinnamon rolls your mother baked but she said they are for after dinner.

2. You lost at a board game with your friends and you want to tip the board over.

3. Your friend Eric wants you to hurry and leave and your dog has not been fed.

4. Sydney asked you to go with her Saturday to a movie you really want to see but you had already made plans to play Barbies with Amber.

5. You strike out at baseball and Josh laughed so you want to quit playing.

6. Dallas beat you in a race and said, "Ha, ha, ha" so you wanted to hit him.

7. Kim told you that her Barbie was prettier than your Barbie so you want to pull Kim's hair.

8. Shad copied your paper so you want to grab his and tear it up.

9. Darla has a note from Shannon that you want to read so you think about grabbing it out of her hands.

10. At home, your brother is bugging you so you think of locking him in the closet.

☑ Lesson 9
Anger Management

> Anger Management – Anger is the feeling you have toward something or someone that hurts, opposes, offends, or annoys you. Management is the ability to handle your anger.

It's okay to feel angry but we all must learn to manage our behavior when we are angry so no one gets hurt. Learning to handle our anger is sometimes hard because sometimes we have our feelings hurt or we are actually hurt physically. Perhaps we once had someone hit us so we hit them back and they hit us back. This goes on until it is a real fight. Then, we might get hurt or lose a friend or get into trouble for fighting. We can learn to manage our behavior when we are angry by learning ways to manage our anger. It is important for us to learn ways to calm down when we're angry so we can think clearly and behave appropriately. It is our responsibility to manage our own anger because no one else can do it for us.

Directions: Discuss the introduction above and teach the steps to anger management:

1. Take three deep breaths and count to 10.
2. Talk about why you are angry.
3. If possible, do an activity that makes you feel calm (a favorite hobby, play a game, ride your bicycle, swing, read).

Discuss how it's your responsibility to know these steps and practice them so you can have the feeling of anger without hurting someone. Stress that all feelings are okay but it is *never, never* okay to hurt someone.

If using puppets, select students to represent the characters in the story and have them lift their puppets up when they hear the name of their character. Tell students to listen to the story so they will be able to tell how Doolee Dog handled his feelings of anger.

Game Time

Billy Goat and Doolee Dog were at Ted Turkey's house one rainy Saturday afternoon. They had been outside playing until the rain came down so hard that Mrs. Turkey called them in. She gave them some hot cocoa and cookies. Then they went into Ted's room and decided to play a game on his computer.

34

"Let's play Space War," said Billy. "I have that game at home and it's loads of fun. Two can play it and the other one can play the winner."

"Hey, all right," said Ted. "I have that game, too. Okay with you, Doolee?"

"Sure. I've never played it but I learn fast," said Doolee. "I'll just watch you two play the first time."

As Billy and Ted played the game, Doolee caught on that the idea was to defeat the other player's side by shooting down all his space ships with one of the two controls. While it was really exciting, it looked pretty easy and Doolee was anxious to try playing it and he said so, but Ted said, "We are using the easy mode now so you can catch on, Doolee. We can set it to be a lot harder."

The two boys kept playing and it did look harder. Both Ted and Billy were yelling and having lots of fun. Then Billy won the game and Doolee said, "Okay, I'm ready to take you on."

"Not yet," said Ted. "We'll show you another level too." Ted and Billy kept on playing. They played for about 15 minutes and Doolee got restless so he went to Ted's Ninjas and started playing with them. Pretty soon, he got tired of that and wandered back to the computer desk but that got boring because he didn't have any fun just watching while the two others were yelling and having a good time.

Finally, Doolee said, "Okay. Hurry up and finish so I can play."

Billy and Ted looked at each other and kept on playing. "We'll be done soon," said Ted.

Doolee stood around some more but he began to get angry. Pretty soon he yelled, "You guys won't ever let me play," and he reached over to push Ted out of the chair. Just then Billy looked up and said, "What are you doing, Doolee? Are you trying to start a fight?"

Doolee realized then he was really angry and he wanted to fight. He felt like hitting Ted or Billy but he remembered to take some deep breaths. He quickly counted to 10 but that didn't help a lot even though Mrs. Giraffe had recently told the class about how to manage anger. He yelled, "You guys are hogging the game! You won't ever let me play!" There, he thought, I told them why I'm angry but I'm still angry. He ran out of the room and slammed the door behind him. He headed to the kitchen to get his coat and go home or do something fun when Mrs. Turkey saw him and said, "Hi, Doolee, sounds like you are a little angry."

"I have to go home," Doolee said just beginning to cool down. He took three more deep breaths and counted to 10 silently as he gathered up his coat and thought I'll work off my anger by riding my bike home.

Mrs. Turkey didn't want him to go home feeling angry so she said, "Can you tell me what's wrong?"

Doolee remembered Mrs. Giraffe said people feel better if they talk about what made them angry so he said, "Ted and Billy won't let me play on the computer with them."

Mrs. Turkey said, "That's too bad and I'm proud of you for not fighting about it. But I hear you can play the piano. I would really like you to play for me. Ted says you play very well. Won't you come into the other room and play our piano."

Doolee really liked playing the piano and he thought that it would be fun to play "Twinkle, Twinkle, Little Star" for Mrs. Turkey. Besides that's the third thing Mrs. Giraffe said to do to get over being angry — do something that makes you feel better and music always made him feel better. So he said, "All right. I guess I can play a song for you but then I have to go home."

Doolee put his coat down and went to the piano thinking playing the piano was more fun than being angry. After he played "Twinkle, Twinkle Little Star" for Mrs. Turkey, they played "Chopsticks" together and then she played the Sunshine School song and they both sang it.

While they were singing it, Ted and Billy came into the room, singing the song along with them.

"Hey, Doolee. We're sorry we didn't let you play Space War. We got involved in the game and didn't realize we were playing so long," said Ted and Billy nodded."Yeah, we're sorry. Maybe we can play a board game that all three of us can play together."

"Right, I have a new game I got for my birthday that I haven't played yet," said Ted. "Let's go to my room and play it."

By this time Doolee felt pretty good, not angry at all. After all Ted and Billy were his friends and he didn't really have to go home for a while so he said, "Okay. Sounds like fun!"

As the three boys walked toward Ted's room, Doolee thought about what Mrs. Giraffe said, "When you learn how to manage your anger, nobody gets hurt and things have a way of working out."

⚠ Discussion Questions

1. What is anger management? (To be able to control your behavior after feeling angry.)

2. Is it all right to feel angry? (Yes)

3. If you are angry is it okay to hurt someone? (No, it is never okay to hurt someone.)

4. What caused Doolee to lose his temper? (Ted and Billy were playing a computer game and left him out.)

5. What did Doolee feel like doing? (He felt like pushing or hitting Ted or Billy.)

6. What did Doolee do? (He took deep breaths and counted to 10 and told them why he was angry.)

7. Did he get over his anger right away? (No, often it is hard to get over anger immediately.)

8. What else did Doolee do to get over his anger? (He left the room and took deep breaths and counted to 10 again. He told Mrs. Turkey about it. Then he played the piano which was something he liked to do.)

9. What are some other things Doolee could have done to control his anger? (He could have gone home and played on his computer, played the piano at home, worked on his hobby, etc.)

10. How did Ted and Billy take responsibility for their actions? (They apologized and suggested playing a board game.)

Activities

1. Have students tell about a time they got angry and what happened as a result. Ask them if they managed their anger and if they didn't, have them discuss what they should have done or would do now that they know the three steps to anger management.

2. Ask the students if they have some other ideas about managing anger and have them share with the class.

3. Have students print the three steps to anger management on a paper and draw a picture that shows how a child is handling a situation that could cause anger. (Option: Post on board or have children explain picture to class.)

Role Play

How would you practice anger management if . . .

1. You are playing a board game when Cory cheats and you feel like throwing the game pieces at him.

2. Your sister ate your piece of pie after school and you are hungry.

3. Your dog chewed up your favorite toy and you want to kick him.

4. Your mother and father tell you they are getting a divorce and you want to hit them.

5. You want to go to the mall with Jody on Saturday and your mother says you have to do the dishes first.

6. Your brother was fooling around and broke your favorite toy so you want to beat him up.

7. Rory and you work on math but you just can't seem to figure out three-number subtraction so you want to wad up your paper and throw it away.

8. Shane accidentally hit you with the ball at recess but it really hurt and you want to take the ball and pound him on the head with it.

9. Carly keeps bumping into you on the playground and laughs about it but she is bigger and sometimes you fall down.

10. Your big sister makes remarks about how dumb you are and you want to hit her.

☑ Lesson 10
"I" Messages

> "I" Messages — "I" Messages are oral or written comments used when we tell how we feel using the word "I" instead of "you."

Using "I" Messages instead of "You" Messages cause others to listen to you and help them understand how you feel. "You" Messages usually place blame or make others feel that you are picking on them. When "You" Messages are given, the other person reacts defensively and with anger. When "I" Messages are given, the other person tends to listen because they are less likely to get angry, so "I" Messages are heard without anger and you are more likely to get what you want. If someone takes your toy and you accuse them or grab it back, they get angry. It is better to say, "I feel sad when you take my toy because I don't have anything to play with." Since you are only telling how you feel, the other person is less likely to get angry and you are more likely to get your toy back.

Directions: Read and discuss introduction. Review what responsible behavior means and have the students give examples. (Do chores, cooperate with others, take charge of our feelings, be honest, practice self-control, and practice anger management.) Ask students what responsibility has to do with knowing how to use "I" Messages. (It is our responsibility to know how to use "I" Messages to cause others to listen to us and help them to understand how we feel. When they understand our feelings we are more likely to get what we want.) Then follow the format below.

Advance preparation: Make two copies of the skit and have a student or adult prepare to read the skit with the teacher.

1. Tell the students there are two ways to express our feelings: "I" Messages and "You" Messages.

2. Explain what "I" Messages are and explain what "You" Messages are (when the speaker places the blame on the "You" and accuses you of doing or saying something that causes the speaker problems or sad feelings, etc.).

3. Write the "I" Message formula on the board or make student copies from Appendix B: I feel _____ when _____ because _____.

4. Give examples of how "I" Messages fit into the formula. (i.e., I feel *hurt* when *you don't talk to me* because *I think you don't like me*. I feel *sad* when *you won't let me play* because *I don't have anyone to play with*.)

5. Give examples of "You" Messages — accuse, criticize, or blame the other person. You don't need to give many examples of "You" Messages because the students al-

ready know how to use those. (You are mean and you never play with me. You always take my toys).

6. Ask the students which of the two ways of expressing yourself sounds better and helps you get what you want, the "I" Messages or the "You" Messages. ("I" Messages)

7. Tell the students you are now going to do two skits involving Polly Pigeon and Minnie Moo.

8. Tell students to listen to the first skit carefully so they will be able to tell if it is an "I" Message skit or a "You" Message skit.

> *Polly:* Minnie, you are so mean! We used to be such good friends and now you never ask me to come play with you. You are always running around with Cherry and Lilly and you never have time for me. You cannot be trusted to be a good friend. You are never dependable. You say you are going to play with me at recess and you never do anymore. I'm never going to be your friend again!

> *Minnie:* Polly, you don't act like you like me anymore! You're the one who's never, ever playing with me. You always run off to play soccer with the boys. You're not dependable. We used to be friends but you don't treat me like a friend anymore. I'm not going to invite you to my house again!

9. Ask the students if this skit shows "I" Messages or "You" Messages. ("You" Messages) How can you tell? (It accuses.)

10. Ask the students what Polly wants from Minnie. (Polly wants Minnie to play with her more.)

11. Will Polly get what she wants using the accusing "You" Messages? (No, accusing and blaming do not usually get you what you want.)

Tell students to listen to the next skit carefully so they will be able to tell if it is an "I" Message or a "You" Message skit.

> *Polly:* Minnie, 1 feel hurt when you go off and play with Cherry and Lilly and don't invite me because I don't have anyone to play with. I feel sad when you treat me like that because I thought you were my friend. Now I feel I can't trust you to be my friend.

> *Minnie:* Polly, I'm sorry. I just got busy with Cherry and Lilly. I want to be your friend and play with you at recess. I'll ask you to play with us from now on. I'll be a good friend because I like you.

10. Ask the students if this skit shows "I" Messages or "You" Messages. ("I" Messages) How can you tell?

11. Which one is better at expressing your feelings? ("I" Messages) Why?

12. Ask students which skit is more likely to get Polly what she wants (to get Minnie to play with her). ("I" Messages. "I" Messages express feelings rather than blaming and accusing.)

▲ Activities

1. Have students brainstorm possible problem situations. (Possible ideas: Your brother always switches the channel when you are watching television, your friend borrows your crayons without asking, your friend takes the ball away from you, your friend kicks you when you are playing soccer, calls you names, crowds in line, pushes you down, gossips about you, hits you with a ball.)

2. In pairs have students role play their situations and use "I" Messages to express their feelings. Teacher will prompt students to use the "I" Message formulas and avoid using *any* "You" Messages in the skits. (Teacher can tell the students that they will not practice the "You" Messages because they already know how to do those.) These may be teacher directed in pairs in front of the class.

3. Draw and color a situation where "I" Messages would help you express your feelings.

☑ Lesson 11
Seeing Both Sides

> Seeing Both Sides – Seeing both sides of an event or discussion means to look at another person's point of view.

When people get into conflict often it is because they don't understand why another person is doing or saying something that they don't agree with or approve of. They must stop and really listen to what the other person is saying or stop and think about why the other person did what they did. Each of us has the responsibility to look at the other person's side of the story in order to solve a conflict.

Directions: Read and discuss the introduction. Review the meaning of responsibility and talk about how conflict often happens because one or both sides have different ideas of what happened. Ask what responsibility has to do with seeing the other person's side of the story. (It is our responsibility to help settle our own conflicts by listening to and seeing the other person's side of the story.) Tell the students to listen to two stories about the same event so they can see and explain both sides. Ask students to raise their hands if they have heard about the story of "Rumpelstiltskin." If a student knows it, ask that student to tell the story. (If none of the students know it, teacher briefly reminds them of the story plot.)

Then the teacher says, "Do you know the beautiful tailor's daughter has been telling her side of the story for years and Rumpelstiltskin says that it's all wrong? First, we're going to hear the girl's side of the story, then we'll hear Rumpelstiltskin's side. Listen so you will be able to hear and understand both sides of the story."

Tailor's Daughter's Side of the Story

Once upon a time, I was just a tailor's daughter helping my dad with the measuring and sewing of clothes for others. Then my dad got me into trouble. He saw the king of our country riding his horse and my dad yelled out that he had a daughter — that's me — who could spin straw into gold. The king stopped and told my dad to bring me to the castle that night so that I could spin straw into gold.

Dad took me to the castle that night and the king put me in a room and told me that if I didn't get all the straw in that room spun into gold by morning I would never see my father again.

This made me cry because I knew I couldn't spin straw into gold. I don't know why my father ever said such a silly thing. I cried and I cried and I cried some more.

42

Poof! Suddenly a funny little man appeared in front of me. I was still crying but the little man said, "I can spin straw into gold. What will you give me if I spin this straw into gold?"

I said I would give him my necklace so he went to work.

The next morning when the king opened the door all the straw was spun into gold. That night the king took me to an even bigger room with even more straw and said I must spin the straw into gold by morning. Again, I sat down and cried in despair.

Again the funny little man appeared and said, "If I spin all this straw into gold, what will you give me?" I said I would give him my gold ring. He got to work and by morning it was done when the king came to the room. The king was happy but greedy and that night he took me to an even bigger room and told me that if I spun all the straw into gold by morning I would become his wife. Again, I sat down and cried in despair.

Again the funny little man appeared and said, "If I spin all this straw into gold, what will you give me?" I didn't have anything more to give so he made me promise to give him my first child after I became queen. Of course, I didn't believe he would really want my child so I said, "Sure, I'll promise you my first-born child."

The next morning the king found the room full of gold so we got married. The next year I gave birth to a beautiful child and that night I was horrified when the little man appeared in my room and wanted my child. I offered him all the treasures of the kingdom but he said, "No."

I cried and begged him not to take my child and finally he said if I could come up with his name in three days, I could keep my child.

After he left, I made a list of all the names I could think of. I even sent a servant out in the kingdom to make a list of all the names he could find in the kingdom.

That first night, the horrible little man came back and asked for me to guess his name. I guessed Tom, Dick, Harry, and more but none of the names were right. The same thing happened the second night. I was getting desperate.

On the third day, I was so upset! I sent the servant out into the kingdom again to see what he could find out. The servant came back and told a story about climbing this really high mountain and finding a little cottage. In front of the cottage was a fire with a little man dancing around it singing a song that went like this: "Today I'll brew, tomorrow I'll bake. Soon I'll have the queen's namesake. Oh, hard it is to play my game for Rumpelstiltskin is my name."

That third night when the little man appeared, I guessed his name as Rumpelstiltskin. He was angry and yelled and screamed but he had to leave without my baby.

(At this point, teacher asks the following questions.)

1. Whose side is being told in this story? (The tailor's daughter)

43

2. What did the tailor tell the King his daughter could do? (Spin straw into gold)

3. Could the tailor's daughter really spin straw into gold? (No)

4. How did the little man help the daughter? (He spun the straw into gold.)

5. What did the little man want after the girl ran out of things to give him? (First-born child)

6. Did the little man get the Queen's (the tailor's daughter) first-born child? (No) Why? (She guessed his name.)

(The teacher says: You've heard one side of the story,
now listen so you can understand another point of view.)

Rumpelstiltskin's Side

First of all, everyone needs to realize that the tailor's daughter who became queen because of the good deeds I did for her is all wrong. For years she has been saying that I was going to take her child but she had promised me that child and I so love children. I really wanted one of my own to bring up and teach all the magic tricks I know. I would have loved that child so very much and given him everything he ever wanted. We would have gone on the most wondrous trips and had the most exciting of adventures. Yet I gave her three chances to break her promise to me because I'm an old softy and when she cried I just had to give her those chances.

In fact, it was her tears that got to me in the first place. She was right. I did help her by spinning the straw into gold, saved her father, and helped her become queen. That necklace and ring she gave were nothing . . . after all, how much could they be worth if a tailor's daughter had them. I really helped her out of the goodness of my heart and she never once said "Thank you" or acted like she appreciated all the help I gave her.

Then she was ready to give me her first-born child. After all, she could have lots of kids and I don't have any. Still, when it came time for her to make good on her promise, she didn't want to do it. So, good-hearted soul that I am, I gave her the chance to keep her child. All she had to do was guess my name and she had all the powers of the kingdom to do it with. I don't know how she found it out but it was probably some underhanded way with a spy or something.

Sure, I got angry when she said my name, but I, at least, kept my promise. I let her keep her child and still that selfish Queen has gone around telling the story as if I am a monster or something. She has really ruined my reputation but I haven't done anything to get even because I am basically a good person. All I want is that someone at least understands my side of the story.

44

⚠ Discussion Questions

1. Whose side is being told in this last story? (Rumpelstiltskin's)

2. Why did he say he helped her by spinning the straw into gold? (Because he is a good person.)

3. Who broke their promise, according to Rumpelstiltskin? (The Queen who once was a tailor's daughter.)

4. Why did Rumpelstiltskin say he wanted the child? (He said he didn't have any children and he would love the child, teach him magic tricks and take him on wondrous adventures.)

5. Why did Rumpelstiltskin tell the queen to guess his name? (He said he did it because she cried.)

6. Did Rukmpelstiltskin keep his promises? (Yes)

7. Tell about a time when someone didn't understand your side of what happened.

8. Tell about a time when you didn't see the other person's side of the story.

🏃 Activities

1. Draw a line across the middle of your paper and on the top draw the Queen's side of the story and on the bottom draw Rumpelstiltskin's side.

2. Tell the class about your picture.

🧎 Role Play

How can you tell both sides of the story if . . .

1. You borrowed Julie's sweater and ripped it accidentally but she thinks you tore it on purpose.

2. Your sister used the remote control and lost it but you think she hid it.

3. You were doing your homework and you forgot to let the cat in for the night and your mom thought you were playing.

4. You played with Jade at recess when you had already promised to play with Dana so she thought you didn't like her.

5. Dakota says she was safe at home plate but you called her out.

6. Shawna got angry when you held two swings because she didn't know you were saving one for Robin.

7. You ate the last piece of pie in the refrigerator then found out it was supposed to be your brother's.

8. You found some change on the floor and spent it on candy but later you found out it belonged to your father.

9. Mike yelled at you and you thought he called you a name so you pushed him.

10. Jake left your bicycle in the driveway and your father got angry with you.

☑ Lesson 12
Resolving Conflicts Peacefully
(Steps to Problem Solving)

> Resolving Conflicts Peacefully — Conflicts occur when two or more people disagree. Solving disagreements peacefully is a win-win situation, not a win-lose situation. This means everyone involved in the conflict is satisfied with the solution.

Resolving conflicts peacefully means each of us involved must take the responsibility to be cooperative and solve the problem. Each person must have a chance to be heard and tell their side of the problem while the others listen. This is not always easy because each of us generally believes that our side is the "right" one. To truly resolve a conflict, each person must stop thinking of their "side" and try to think of the other person's "side." The five steps to problem solving can help each of us do this.

Directions: Discuss the introduction then read the following steps to solving the problem or conflict peacefully (see steps in Appendix B):

1. If you are angry, take three deep breaths and count to 10.

2. Each person states the problem. (No interrupting, name calling, or physical contact.)

3. Brainstorm solutions. (Together)

4. Choose a solution that is fair to all parties. (Win-win)

5. Follow through with the solution.

Discuss how it's our responsibility to know these steps and practice them so we can learn to resolve conflicts peacefully. If using puppets select the students to represent the characters in the story. The teacher then tells the students to listen to the story and see how Minnie Moo and Susie Squirrel resolve their conflict.

Playing With Barbie

One Saturday afternoon Minnie Moo and Susie Squirrel were having great fun playing with their Barbies at Susie's house. Minnie had brought her brand new Birthday Barbie that she got for her birthday last week. Susie had Butterfly Barbie, the Barbie house, and fancy car. They had both Barbies finish cleaning the house and go for a ride. After the ride, when both girls handled the remote control avoiding any serious Barbie accident, Mrs. Squirrel called to the girls and said, "Minnie, your mom just called on the phone and she will be here to pick you up in 10 minutes."

Susie and Minnie didn't really want to end the playtime because they were having so much fun. Susie said, "Minnie, could you leave your Birthday Barbie here to play with mine until Monday? I'll bring her to school for you then."

"I guess so," said Minnie. "My family is going to the beach Sunday so I won't have time to play with her anyway. Just don't forget to bring her Monday, okay?"

"I promise," said Susie.

But when Monday came along, Susie forgot to bring Minnie's Birthday Barbie to school. She ran up to Minnie that morning and said, "I forgot your Barbie today. I'm sorry. I promise to bring it tomorrow."

Tuesday, Susie forgot again but this time she stayed far away from Minnie because she felt embarrassed.

Wednesday the same thing happened and Susie didn't go near Minnie at any recess or after school, even though Minnie, when she thought of it, would look for Susie.

By Thursday Minnie was getting really angry and finally found Susie on the playground and yelled, "Susie, you are a stealer. You kept my Birthday Barbie and I want it back!"

Susie yelled right back, "I can't help it if I keep forgetting."

Minnie yelled, "That's a dumb excuse. You promised you would bring it to school Monday. I might believe that you forgot one day but not all week, you stealer!"

All the girls' friends heard Susie and Minnie yelling and gathered around.

Kathy Kat, who is a very good problem solver, said, "Hey, you guys, stop yelling at each other and use the problem solving steps our teacher taught us. Remember, the first one is to take three deep breaths and count to 10 to calm down. Here I'll breathe with you. One . . . two . . . three . . . now, let's count to 10 . . . one . . . two . . . three . . ."

By the time the three girls took three breaths and had counted to 10, Susie and Minnie were fairly calm.

As they remembered the steps the teacher taught them, first Minnie, then Susie each told the problem.

Minnie said, "I left my Birthday Barbie at your house so you could play with it. You promised you'd bring it to school for me on Monday."

Susie said, "My side of the problem is you called me a stealer and yelled at me."

Kathy said, "Okay, you guys, you each said your side of the problem. Now it's time to brainstorm a solution. We can help you come up with some ideas."

*(Option: The teacher has the option to stop the story at this point
and have students come up with possible solutions.)*

Second Grade, Lesson 12: Resolving Conflicts Peacefully

Minnie, Susie, Kathy, and several of their friends came up with some possible solutions.

"Minnie, you could go home with Susie and get your Barbie," said Lilly Lambkin.

"Susie, you could tie a string around your finger to help you remember to bring the Barbie to school and Minnie, you could apologize for calling Susie names," suggested Polly Pigeon.

"Susie and Minnie, you two could go to the beach and play with your Barbies," said Ted Turkey.

"Susie could keep the Barbie and buy Minnie a new one," suggested Corky Colt.

"Minnie could just give Susie the Barbie and not speak to her again," said Doolee Dog.

"You two could fight," suggested Billy Goat.

Kathy looked at the two girls and said, "You have a lot of suggestions. Are you going to use one of them or are you going to make up one of your own?"

Susie and Minnie looked at each other and Minnie started laughing. "Well, I don't really want to fight Susie. I just want my Barbie, but I think my part of the solution is that I should apologize for calling you names, Susie. I'm sorry."

Those were good suggestions you guys gave but I want to make up my own solution. I will call my mother. I'll ask her to bring your Barbie with her when she picks me up after school."

Kathy looked at both girls and said, "Do you both agree to this solution?"

"Yes," both girls said.

After school when Mrs. Squirrel handed Susie Minnie's Birthday Barbie, Susie said, "Why don't we play Barbies on Saturday, Minnie?"

"That'd be great," said Minnie. "Let's play at my house and my mother will make brownies and we can take our Barbies on a picnic."

⚠ Discussion Questions

1. What started the conflict? (Susie didn't return Minnie's Barbie.)

2. What did Minnie do to Susie? (She called her names.)

3. How did the two feel about the problem? (Mad)

4. What were the steps they used to resolve the conflict?

    •   Took three deep breaths and counted to 10 to calm down. (1)

    •   Each stated the problem from her point of view. (2)

- They brainstormed solutions. (3)
- Minnie and Susie chose a win-win solution. (4)
- They did it. (5)

5. Did the characters resolve the conflict the way our class suggested?

6. Does anyone want to tell about a recent conflict they had and how it was resolved? Did you use the steps to resolving the conflict peacefully? If not, what happened? How could such a result be prevented next time?

✗ Activities

1. Draw a picture about a playground conflict and how it could be resolved.
2. Draw a poster showing the five steps to resolving conflicts peacefully

🙎 Role Play

How would you use the steps to resolving conflicts peacefully if . . .

1. Every time Jordan walks by your house he kicks your dog, so you call him a name.
2. Your brother grabs your toy and you push him.
3. When June comes over to play, she always talks about how much fun she has with her other friends, so you tell her to go home.
4. Paul and you are playing a board game and he cheats, so you turn the game board over.
5. You signed up to take the ball out at recess and Bob grabs it, so you push him down and take the ball.
6. Your sister calls you names and you mess up her room.
7. Your best friend, Libby, invites you to the movies then takes someone else, so you won't play with her.
8. Rick keeps interrupting your group's discussion, so you put your hand over his mouth.
9. Lou keeps telling all your friends that you love Dave, so you call her a name.
10. Len keeps cutting in line in front of you so you throw mud at him.

☑ Lesson 13
Being a Good Friend

> Being a Good Friend — Being a good friend is being able to appreciate another person and enjoy being around them and to practice friendly behavior so that they appreciate you and want to be around you.

It is our responsibility to learn how to be a good friend. It is important to understand that the things we want in a friend are also the same things others want in a friend. If we want others to be friends with us, we must practice friendly behavior ourselves. Here are some keys to practicing friendly behavior:

1. Treat friends with kindness (like you want them to treat you).

2. Make friends feel special (listen to them, share with them, notice their feelings, be encouraging, and let them have other friends).

3. Be trustworthy with friends (keep promises, keep secrets, be loyal, be honest).

Using these keys to friendly behavior will help you get and keep friends. A good friend is caring, fair, helpful, honest, kind, and fun. A good friend is also willing to share and is a good sport. When you are sad, a good friend will listen to you and help you feel better. When you want to play games, a good friend will play fair, cheer you on, and never cheat. If they do lose in a game, they are good sports even when they aren't happy about losing. A good friend will share their candy with you. A good friend is fun to be with.

Directions: Tell students that today the lesson will be on friendship and how to be a good friend. Ask students why it is important to have friends (everyone needs someone else to play with and talk to). Ask what responsibility has to do with being a good friend. (It is our responsibility to know what to do to be a good friend.) Read and discuss the introduction with students and write the three keys to friendly behavior on the board or on a chart.

Advance Preparations: On the next pages are two skits that use the Sunshine Elementary puppets. Copy each skit and select students or adult helpers for each skit. If using students, have them practice the skits in advance then have them read the skits for the rest of the class. Tell the class to listen to the skits and decide which skit shows friendly behavior and which one shows unfriendly behavior. You may wish to make up more of your own skits to further illustrate the three keys to friendly behavior. For Skit 1 "A Secret" tell the students to listen to discover if Lilly Lambkin uses friendly or unfriendly behavior.

Skit 1 – A Secret

Minnie Moo (crying):	I'm so sad.
Lilly Lambkin:	Oh, you big baby, what are you crying about now?
Minnie:	I really need to talk to you. I feel really bad.
Lilly:	Oh, I guess you can but hurry up, I want to go jump rope with Susie.
Minnie:	My parents are getting a divorce.
Lilly:	That's too bad. Come on, let's go jump rope.
Minnie:	I don't know, I feel bad.
Lilly:	Get over it. Grown-ups do weird things.
Minnie:	I guess you're right. Please don't tell anyone.
Lilly:	Okay.
Cherry (later that day at recess):	Why do you suppose Minnie is so sad today?
Lilly:	Minnie's folks are getting a divorce.

⚠? Questions

1. Did this skit illustrate friendly or unfriendly behavior? (Unfriendly)

2. Using the three keys to friendly behavior (see introduction to lesson), name the unfriendly behaviors that Lilly used. (Didn't seem to care, wanted to go play, told someone else, etc.)

3. How do you think Minnie felt when Lilly was using unfriendly behavior? (Sad and hurt)

4. How could Lilly have shown friendly behavior? (Use the three keys to friendly behavior.)

*(Tell students to listen to Skit 2 "Play Ball" so they can tell
if Doolee Dog uses friendly or unfriendly behavior.)*

Skit 2 - Play Ball

Ronnie Rabbit:	Do we have to play ball today?
Doolee Dog:	Sure, come on. It's really fun.
Ronnie:	That's easy for you to say. You're good. You can hit the ball.
Doolee:	You can hit the ball, too.
Ronnie:	How?
Doolee:	When the ball comes at you, keep your eye on it until your bat hits the ball.
Ronnie:	What?
Doolee:	Come on. I'll show you. See, I'll toss the ball to you and you watch it until you hit it with your bat.
Ronnie:	Okay.
Doolee:	That's right. Here the ball comes.
Ronnie:	I missed.
Doolee:	Here it comes again.
Ronnie:	Wow! I hit it!
Doolee:	See, I told you you could do it.
Ronnie:	Yeah!
Doolee:	Let's go play ball with the rest of the kids now.
Ronnie:	You bet!

⚠ Questions

1. Did this skit illustrate friendly or unfriendly behavior? (Friendly)

2. Using the three keys to friendly behavior, name the friendly behaviors (see introduction to lesson).

3. How do you think Ronnie felt when Doolee was using friendly behavior? (Answers vary)

✗ Activities

1. Make a poster by decorating it with a colorful combination of friendly words (caring, helpful, good listener, etc.) and happy designs (stars, hearts, rainbows, etc.).

2. Draw a picture showing a time when you were a good friend. Share it with the class and tell how you felt. How do you think your friend felt?

3. Write a paragraph about a time a friend used unfriendly behavior with you. Be sure to include how you felt.

✗ Role Play

Refer to the three keys to friendly behavior (1. treat friends with kindness, 2. make friends feel special, 3. be trustworthy with friends).

How would you show friendly behavior if . . .

1. Wendy wants to include Kathy in plans to go to the movies with Wendy and you.

2. You're in the lunch line and Ana says she's really hungry.

3. You notice Ben is having trouble with his art project.

4. Ashley did something you thought was really neat.

5. Jimmy missed the ball and the other players started to call him names like klutz.

6. You brought a bag of cookies for a snack and you notice Mike doesn't have a snack.

7. You see Jan on the playground and you would really like to get to know her better.

8. You have several Halloween costumes and Diana doesn't have any.

9. You promise Dan that he can go camping with your family and Doug, your favorite cousin, shows up to go camping.

10. You are playing a computer game with Debbie and you really want to win. Debbie feels very proud when she wins.

☑ Lesson 14
Listening Is Important

Listening Is Important — Listening is important because when we pay attention to what someone says, we can respond to their comment. It's valuable also to pay attention so we do not miss some necessary information.

It is our responsibility to be a good listener. The three keys to being a good listener are:

1. Look at the person talking.

2. Do not interrupt.

3. Show you are listening by saying "wow" or "great" or asking questions or making comments about what the speaker said.

Some of the reasons we all need to be good listeners include: We can discover things about others, we can show our friends we care about them and their activities and by listening we show them the same respect as we want them to give us. Listening also holds the key to learning. Being a good listener helps us learn from others, particularly our teachers. Learning to be good listeners will help us become good students.

Directions: Review what students have been learning about responsible behavior and have students name some examples. (Do chores, listen to both sides of a story, use "I" messages, be honest, and practice self-control.) Ask them what responsibility has to do with being a good listener? (It is our responsibility to practice being a good listener.) Discuss the introduction and teach the keys to good listening that are listed above. Then, ask the following questions.

1. What have you learned people should do to show they are good listeners? (Look at the person speaking, listen to what the speaker is saying, don't interrupt, and give responses that show you are listening.)

2. How do you learn to be a good listener? (Practice the three keys to being a good listener.)

3. Why does being a good listener mean you are showing responsibility? (Because it shows you care about others and what they are saying.)

If using puppets select students to represent the characters in the story and have them stand where they can be seen by other students. After giving out the puppets, explain that when they hear their character talk in the story they are to raise the puppet so the other students can see which animal is talking. Tell the students to listen to the story so they will be able to tell what the second graders at Sunshine Elementary learned about being good listeners.

Listening Is Important

It was after morning recess and the students in Mrs. Giraffe's class were in groups working on some math games. In Lilly Lambkin's group were Cherry Chicken, Ronnie Rabbit, and Doolee Dog. They were using flash cards and taking turns holding the cards. Everyone had to hold up their hand before giving the answer but Lilly wasn't waiting. She insisted on yelling out the answer all the time.

"Lilly," said Cherry. "You have to hold up . . .

"I know, I know," said Lilly interrupting Cherry. But Lilly was even more talkative than usual that day and she kept doing it.

After the flash-card game, the group had to decide which math game they wanted to play but no one got to say anything except Lilly. She kept interrupting everyone and telling them what she wanted to do. Finally, Ronnie said, "We're never going to decide because . . ."

Again Lilly interrupted, "I already told you guys what we should do." But everyone just groaned.

Then Mrs. Giraffe came to the group and said, "What's going on over here? It sounds like you are having trouble."

"Mrs. Giraffe, Lilly won't listen and she's talking all . . . " started Doolee, but Lilly interrupted, "That's not true, Mrs. Giraffe. They won't listen."

Just then the noon recess bell rang. Lilly was still talking as she and Cherry stood in line for their hot lunch, "Let's play with our Barbies after lunch. Okay?"

But before Cherry had a chance to point out that Lilly was the only one who had brought her Barbie, she saw that Lilly was not listening because she was busy telling about the television program she saw last night. Cherry gave up. Lilly wasn't paying attention to anything Cherry was saying.

Outside on the playground, Lilly brought out her Barbie but no one else had brought theirs so she said, "I thought we were all going to bring our Barbies today."

"You weren't listening when we said we wanted to play kick ball today," said Kathy Kat. "We all agreed that we would bring our Barbies next . . . " But she didn't even get her sentence finished before Lilly turned to Susie Squirrel and said, "Why didn't you tell me?"

"We did," said Susie but, of course, Lilly didn't hear that because she was showing Polly Pigeon her new Barbie doll.

That afternoon, Lilly continued to do most of the talking in her group and when the class was supposed to be listening to a story during reading, she whispered to Ted Turkey about the story. Both Ted and Lilly got a stern look from Mrs. Giraffe.

The next few days, much the same thing happened. Lilly was starting to get her friends angry at her and at recess one day Cherry and Kathy were talking.

"What on earth has happened to Lilly? She is so rude. She never listens to anybody." said Kathy.

"I don't know," said Cherry. "But somebody had better tell her to cool it or she will lose all of us as friends. It's like she has no respect for what we have to say because she keeps interrupting and pays no attention to us when we talk."

"You tell her," suggested Kathy.

"I will if she interrupts me one more time," said Cherry.

Just then Lilly came up with her Barbie doll, "Hey, you guys, I thought today was the day we were going to play with our Barbies. Where are yours?"

Cherry said, "Lilly, we told you last week that we were going to . . . "

"Why didn't you bring yours?" interrupted Lilly.

"That does it," said Cherry. "You haven't listened to anybody for the last week. You are . . . " Just then Lilly tied to interrupt but Cherry kept going and Lilly had to listen. "You haven't shown us any respect and you don't even pay attention when we are talking. We want to be your friends, but you must be our friend, too," Cherry said.

This time Lilly heard what Cherry had to say and she looked shocked. "Have I really been that bad?" she asked.

"Yes," said Cherry and Kathy together.

"Oh, wow! I was wondering why everyone wasn't talking to me very much or playing with me. It wasn't them, was it? It was me." Lilly said sadly. "I do like you guys a lot. What can I do to make up for hurting your feelings?"

"You can look at us when we talk and not interrupt," said Cherry. "Remember that those are two of the keys to being a good listener that we learned last year."

"And you can even remember to nod your head and make some nice comments, like 'that's great' or 'wow.' That shows you are really listening," said Kathy.

"Okay," said Lilly, being very careful to look each of the others in the eye while they were talking. "You are great friends to help me."

Just to be sure Lilly really meant it, Cherry started telling the two girls about her fun weekend at her aunt's house, sort of pausing to see if Lilly would interrupt. No way! Lilly looked Cherry in the eyes and said, "Wow! What a great time you had, Cherry," then she waited for Cherry to keep talking.

58

Lilly really was going to practice being a good listener rather than a good talker because she liked her friends and it was really important to her to be a super good friend.

⚠ Discussion Questions

1. Why did Lilly's friends get upset with her? (She would not listen to them.)

2. What are the three keys to good listening? (Look at the person talking; do not interrupt; show you are listening by saying "wow" or "great.")

3. How did Lilly finally get the message that she was being rude and not listening to her friends? (Cherry and Kathy told her and reminded her of the three keys to good listening.)

4. Tell about a time that a friend wouldn't listen to you. What happened? How did you feel?

5. Tell about a time that you didn't listen to something important that a friend said. What happened?

🏃 Activities

1. Have students draw a picture using one of the three keys to good listening.

2. Have students share their picture with the class.

🙇 Role Play

Remember to have students practice the three keys to listening. (1. Look at the person talking, 2. do not interrupt, 3. show you are listening by making comments about what they said.)

How would you show you were listening if . . .

1. School is starting and you really want to tell Kelly about your vacation, but she starts talking about her trip to Canada.

2. You know the story your teacher is reading to the class and you want to tell Sara about the ending.

3. David is telling Luke about the fish he caught with his dad and you want to tell about the one you caught.

4. You think you know the rules for soccer and you want to tell the new kid while the captain is talking.

5. Shaylee is telling the class about her trip to Mexico and you want to tell about your trip to Florida.

6. You saw an exciting movie last night and you want to tell Joan but she is talking about her friend who is visiting from out of town.

7. You want to share about your bike ride when the teacher talks about the qualities it takes to be a world-class, cross-country bike rider.

8. Your mother is telling you when to be home tomorrow but you are trying to tell her about the tricks that your dog did.

9. Your older sister is baby-sitting you and she is giving you instructions about going to bed but you are watching television.

10. Your brother told you where to get the soap to help wash his car but you are playing in the water.

☑ Lesson 15
Playing Fair

> Playing Fair — To play fair means to follow the rules and not to cheat or change the rules and to always act honorably whether you win or lose.

It is our responsibility to play fair when playing with others. If we want others to trust us and continue to play with us, then we will always follow the rules, take our turn when it is really our turn, and not try to change the rules in the middle of the game. Winning is fun, but it is not worth cheating or losing friends. Playing fair means that we try our best to win, but we know that it is not always possible to win so we try not to get upset when we lose because we know there will always be another game to play. It is important to play fair because we should think about our friends and how we would feel if they didn't play fair. Others lose respect for us if we continually whine about losing or we continually try to get extra turns or crowd into a line. Playing fair is an important part of our responsibility to ourselves and to others.

Directions: Read and discuss the introduction. Ask students what they have learned about responsible behavior and have them give some examples. (Do chores, listen to both sides of a story, use "I" messages, be honest, and practice self-control.) Ask what responsibility has to do with playing fair. (It is our responsibility to think of others and play fair because we know how we would feel if someone didn't play fair with us.) For the lesson, if using puppets have students hold up puppets when characters' names are mentioned so other students can see the character who is talking. Tell students to listen carefully to the story so they will be able to tell what the second graders from Sunshine Elementary School learned about playing fair.

Playing Games

One rainy Saturday afternoon, Ronnie Rabbit was at Billy Goat's house and the two boys were going to play checkers. Ronnie said he liked the game because his grandfather, Peter Rabbit, taught him how to play.

Billy's grandfather, Big Billy Goat, had also taught young Billy how to play. "My gramps was tough and that's why I'm named after him," Billy boasted to Ronnie after Ronnie told him his gramps had stories written about him. Both boys laughed and Ronnie said, "Well, guess we are both good checkers players."

61

They started playing and were having great fun. It looked like Billy had more kings and had taken more of Ronnie's checkers when Billy laughed and said, "This is fun and I'm going to win this game."

"Oh, no," said Ronnie. "I was taught by the best so I will win." But he didn't.

The second game was different. Ronnie was playing really well and he got the first king and took the first checker from Billy. Before long Ronnie had cornered Billy's last king, jumped it, and won the game.

Mrs. Goat brought in some punch and cookies and the boys took a break. "Let's play a different board game," suggested Billy. "I'm getting bored with checkers."

"I'm not," said Ronnie. "Besides we have to play another game so we can to see who's the champion."

"Well, okay," said Billy as he set up his black checkers again.

After the first few moves, the boys had each lost a few checkers and each friend had gained one king. They appeared to be about even but both boys got serious and were determined to win and be champion.

After Billy jumped one of Ronnie's red checkers and made another black king, Ronnie snarled and twisted his nose at Billy as kids do when they are getting upset. Billy didn't notice at all. But he suddenly stood up and said, "I'll be right back. I have to go get a drink."

After Billy left the room, Ronnie sat and stared at the board. He saw a couple of places that he could jump Billy's checkers and even get a king, if Billy moved one checker just right. He sighed and thought Billy will never do that. Then he reached out and moved the black checker.

Just then Billy came back into the room, yelling, "You moved my checker. That's cheating. Put the checker back. How would you like it if I moved your checker?"

Ronnie tried to say he hadn't moved the checker, but Billy said, "I was just coming into the room and I saw you do it. If you don't put it back, I won't play with you any more."

Ronnie stood up with his hands on his hips and said, "No, I didn't move the checker. I'm going home." And he did.

The next week at school, Ronnie avoided Billy at recesses and Billy didn't mind even though they had always been good friends and played together a lot.

Friday, they were on the same kick ball team and had to stand together. Ronnie looked at Billy and said, "I've missed playing with you."

"Me, too," said Billy. "But I can't play with a cheater."

"I guess I didn't play fair that day. I'm really sorry I moved your checker. I really wanted to win but I think friends are more important than winning," Ronnie said hanging his head. "I know I wouldn't like it if you had moved my checker. I'm really sorry. I promise I'll play fair from now on."

Billy said, "I accept your apology but it's going to be a while before I trust you again. Friends are supposed to play fair and cheer each other on instead of cheating and I thought we were friends."

Just then it was Billy's turn to kick the ball and as he went up to the base, Ronnie cheered for him.

⚠ Discussion Questions

1. What were Billy Goat and Ronnie Rabbit doing that Saturday afternoon? (Playing checkers)

2. Who won? (Billy won the first game, Ronnie won the second game, and they didn't finish the third game.)

3. Why didn't they finish the third game of checkers? (Because Billy caught Ronnie moving his black checker.)

4. That Saturday, did Ronnie admit that he wasn't playing fair? (No)

5. Did Ronnie ever apologize for cheating? (Yes) Why? (He missed playing with his friend.)

6. Have you ever played with someone who wasn't playing fair? How did you feel?

7. Tell about a time that you didn't play fair? How do you think your friend felt?

🏃 Activities

1. Draw a picture of students playing a game and color the one who is not playing fair.

2. Draw a picture of students playing a game and color the ones who are playing fair.

🧎 Role Play

Note: Be sure to bring in empathy by discussing how the characters feel when others are not playing fair.

What would you do if . . .

1. Joe and you are playing basketball and he keeps talking to other children, so you are thinking of taking extra turns.

2. You are playing a board game with you brother and he keeps taking extra game money.

3. Playing kick ball, Jon put you out at second base, but you want to say you were safe.

4. You are in line to go down the slide and Jill pushes in front of you.

5. You are playing a board game with your little sister and you want to change the rules in your favor.

6. You are playing hide-and-seek and you are thinking of hiding outside the boundaries.

7. It is your turn to jump rope because Tara missed, but she keeps jumping.

8. It is your turn to be on the computer, but Ken wants to take your turn.

9. It is your turn to choose the Ninja game, but Ted refuses to play if he can't choose the game.

10. Playing softball you have three strikes but you want to keep batting.

☑ Lesson 16
Feeling Left Out

Feeling Left Out — Feeling left out is when you are not invited to play or join in games or other activities and it makes you feel sad.

It is our responsibility to have what we call empathy for others and invite them to play when they are feeling left out. Empathy means to understand how others feel or understand how you would feel if you were in their place. Students who come to a new school often feel left out until someone invites them to join their group of friends. Others might feel left out if they are not included in a game, party, or group activity. Being able to see when people feel left out is important. Someone standing alone and looking sad might mean the person is feeling left out. It is our responsibility to go talk to them or include them in what we are doing. We need to be able to understand how they are feeling because we know how we would feel if we were in their place. No one likes to be left out but all of us have felt that way once in a while. We can also take the responsibility of going up to a group or a friend and asking to join them if we feel left out.

Directions: Read and discuss the introduction and briefly review what students have been learning about responsible behavior. Have students give examples of responsible behavior. (Do chores, listen to both sides of a story, use "I" messages, be honest, and practice self-control.) Discuss what responsibility has to do with helping people feel a part of a group. (It is our responsibility to have empathy for others and invite them to play so they don't feel left out.) Discuss how to recognize when people are feeling left out. Tell students to look around them and if they see a student who is standing away from others and no one is talking to them, then they are probably feeling alone and left out. Sometimes this means we will have to leave our group and go over to the person. It can be rewarding because we may find a new friend who is fun to play with. Listen carefully to the story so you will be able to tell how the "ugly duckling" felt about being left out.

The Ugly Duckling

Once upon a time there was a mother duck who laid six lovely eggs. She was so proud when the first five beautiful ducklings hatched. But one egg, the biggest, took a little longer to hatch and when it did, out toddled the largest, ugliest duckling the mother had ever seen. Now, she tried very hard to think he was beautiful, but when she took her family for a walk around the barnyard the next morning, the other barnyard animals exclaimed, "What a fine family, except for that huge ugly one at the end." The most fancy looking duck in the barnyard said, "Keep that ugly one away from me."

Because the barnyard animals wouldn't accept him, the ugly duckling's brothers and sisters soon turned against him. One of his brothers even said, "I wish the cat would take you." The ugly duckling asked, "Why can't you accept me as I am?" But his brothers and sisters continued to pick and peck and tease him. Even his mom began to push him into the background whenever she went visiting or took the youngsters for a swim.

The ugly duckling became very sad, and one day after being left out of the family fun, he decided he might as well go off on his own since no one would care. He ran away but as he left the barnyard, he fell off the fence and landed in a flock of songbirds who called him a "monster" and flew off. He was left alone again.

As the ugly duckling wandered through a grassy field, he came upon a flock of geese. He wondered if the geese would accept him. But as he tried to make friends with them, he heard shots from hunters' rifles that scattered the flock and he was alone again, hiding in the tall weeds.

(Option: Teacher may stop here and discuss the following questions.)

1. How did the ugly ducking look different than his brothers and sisters? (He was bigger and didn't look like a duck.)

2. Why did they leave him out and pick on him? (He looked different.)

3. How did the ugly duckling feel about being left out? (Sad, alone, and unloved)

4. What did he do? (Ran away)

5. What do you think will happen to the ugly duckling?

(Continue reading)

The ugly duckling spent the winter in a small secluded pond all by himself. It was a long cold winter and he felt more left out and alone than ever. As the pond began to melt, the ugly duckling saw some beautiful birds with magnificent wings flying over. He thought how wonderful it would be to make friends with them but he felt these graceful beings would only run from him, too.

As spring came on, the ugly duckling felt himself changing and growing and one day as he stretched his wings to feel the warm sun on them, he lifted into the air and discovered that he could fly. He had great fun soaring in the wind then he landed in a beautiful lake. Nearby swam three beautiful, long-neck birds which he recognized as the elegant creatures he had seen before. He was sure they would chase him away, but they bowed their long necks in a friendly greeting. When he bowed, too, he caught a reflection of himself in the clear, blue lake and saw with amazement that he looked just like the other three birds.

Then, he heard a little girl on the bank squeal, "Look, a new swan! Even more beautiful than the rest!"

The ugly duckling had grown into a beautiful swan and proudly joined the flock but he never allowed the beautiful birds to make others feel left out just because they were different.

⚠ Discussion Questions

1. Did the story end like you thought it would?
2. How did the ugly duckling discover he wasn't a duck? (Found the other swans)
3. How did he feel when he discovered he was a swan? (Happy and not left out anymore)
4. Tell about a time that you were left out? How did you feel?
5. Tell about a time when you left someone out. How do you think they felt?

Activity

Divide students into groups of three or four to draw and color a collage about the "Ugly Duckling" using a large piece of butcher paper. Give directions that everyone in the group must be included. No one is to be left out in the decision-making or the drawing. After the groups are done, have them discuss whether or not everyone participated. Picture may be posted in room.

Role Play

How would you handle a situation to avoid making others feel left out, if . . .

1. A new boy came to school and everyone ignored him at recess.
2. Jill is sitting alone on the stairs and you see three of her friends walking by, whispering.
3. Tristan wants to play kick ball and the others on the team won't let him.
4. A new girl got teased because she looked different.
5. Tom broke his leg so he can't play a lot of the games.
6. Sara was planning to go to the movies with Debbie, but Debbie took another friend instead.
7. Your brother and his friend are playing a game and won't let your little brother play.
8. Two big boys are teasing Tim.
9. On a Friday night, your sister is home because she didn't get invited to her friend's party.
10. The captains are picking people for kick ball teams but Brian doesn't get chosen.

☑ Lesson 17
Handling Bullies

Handling Bullies — A bully is someone who teases, frightens, threatens, harasses, intimidates, or hurts smaller or weaker people. Handling means using ways to deal with a bully.

Handling bullies takes the ability to think clearly without reacting in an emotional way. If you cry, yell, or act scared, this encourages the bully because that's what he wants you to do. You must always take the responsibility for your actions but you must remember that you are not responsible for a bully's behavior. His threatening behavior is always his problem, not yours. There are some steps you can take to help you handle the way a bully treats you: (1) Ignore the bully and walk away. (2) Assert yourself: Stand tall and look them in the eye and say, "Stop it! I don't like it when you treat me that way." (3) Ask for help from an adult if the bully continues threatening you or hurts you. (4) Self talk: Tell yourself, "It's the bully's problem and I'm okay."

Directions: Read and discuss introduction. Ask students what they have been learning about responsibility and have them give examples of responsible behavior. (Take responsibility for your behavior, cooperate with others, be respectful, control your anger, practice conflict resolution.) Ask what responsibility has to do with handling a bully. (It is our responsibility to know how to handle a bully so we can take care of ourselves and our feelings.) Tell the students to listen to the story so they will be able to tell what the animal friends learn about handling bullies.

Corky Colt's Birthday Party

It was a beautiful, bright, spring day in Anytown, USA. It was Saturday and there seemed to be a lot of light-hearted activity among all the townsfolk, kind of like bears coming out of hibernation after a long, cold winter. All the townspeople were out shopping or working in their yards and pleasantly chatting about how they were enjoying the nice sunny day.

All the friends from second grade were practically jumping for joy; it was such a nice day and they were invited to the city park for Corky Colt's birthday party. After everyone had arrived, Lilly and Lucky Lambkin, who were in charge of activities, got a game of "Duck, Duck, Goose" going. Since it was Corky's special day, he got to chose the first person to be "it." He picked Ted Turkey who was thrilled to be first around the circle because he didn't get picked for anything very often. Ted began touching heads, saying, "Duck, Duck, Duck, Duck" and then got ready to run fast as he touched Cherry Chicken on the head and yelled "Goose." All the children squealed with laughter as the game got more and more exciting with each one taking a turn at being "it" and trying to beat the youngster playing "goose" back to his space in the circle.

After the exhilarating game of "Duck, Duck, Goose" wound down, the animals all lined up to play a challenging game of horseshoes. Lilly, with her fluffy white head bobbing, explained, "The object of the game is to make points by throwing the horse shoe so it rings around the steel peg that sticks out of the ground."

Some were really good at getting ringers and others, like Minnie Moo, who had never played before had fun trying. The friends, all having a great time, whooped and hollered and cheered for one another. Then it was Corky's turn to try to make a ringer. As he stepped up to the line, Susie Squirrel accidentally bumped Corky's arm and caused the horseshoe to go flying over toward a ball field where a lot of older boys were playing.

Everyone was astonished when Bart Bull, a big sixth grader, came running over with his hands clenched like he was going to fight. He got right in Corky's face and said, "You throw horseshoes like a baby. You almost hit me and it would have been a big mistake to make me angry. You never know what I'll do when I'm angry."

Corky tried to apologize but Bart wouldn't listen. It looked like he was acting tough to show off for his friends. Corky was really upset so the birthday party ended early.

After that day every time Bart saw Corky at school, he tried to intimidate him by calling him names, pushing him around, taking his money, or making Corky carry his books. Corky was really scared of Bart and when he came close, Corky hung his head, slumped his shoulders, and did everything Bart commanded him to do. He was not sleeping, eating, or paying attention to his lessons at school. His good friend, Ted Turkey, wanted to help, so he said, "Corky, do you want to come over to my house and talk with my dad about your problem? He is really good at helping."

Corky thought that was a good idea, so the two friends headed over to Ted's house after school. When they explained to Ted's father that Bart was behaving like a bully to Corky, he said, "I went to school with a mule in junior high who treated me just like that and I'll tell you what the school counselor taught me to do to handle a bully: 1. Ignore him and walk away. 2. Assert yourself: Stand tall and look him in the eye and say, 'Stop it! I don't like it when you treat me that way.' 3. If the bully chooses to continue to call you names or threaten you, ask for help from an adult. 4. Self talk: Tell yourself, 'That's the bully's problem, I'm okay.' Do you think you can do all of the steps? You have already done the third one by talking with me."

"Yes, I do," replied Corky. "I have to try. I feel so sad and embarrassed all the time the way it is now."

The next day the students at Sunshine Elementary crowded around as Corky bravely crossed the school yard toward Bart. With his new found confidence Corky marched straight up to Bart, while Bart was calling him names, and said, "Stop calling me names and pushing me around. I don't like it and I'm not going to take it anymore."

When Corky turned and walked away he heard the other students cheering for him. As Corky strutted away he told himself, "Bart is the one with the problem, I'm really okay."

The next few weeks Bart tried several times to bully Corky, but Corky stood tall and ignored him so eventually Bart left Corky alone.

⚠️ Discussion Questions

1. What happened to ruin Corky's birthday party? (Bart got angry and bullied Corky.)

2. How did Corky react? (He let Bart bully him.)

3. Did Bart continue to harass Corky? (Yes) How? (Called him names, threatened him, made him carry his books, etc.)

5. What did Corky learn from Ted Turkey's dad? (How to deal with a bully)

6. What are the steps he learned? (1) Ignore the bully and walk away. (2) Assert yourself: Stand tall and look them in the eye and say, "Stop it! I don't like it when you treat me that way." (3) Ask for help from an adult if the bully continues threatening you or hurts you. (4) Self talk: Tell yourself, "It's the bully's problem and I'm okay."

7. Did Corky try the steps on Bart? (Yes) What happened? (Bart eventually left him alone.)

🏃 Activities

1. Draw a picture of a time when someone behaved like a bully toward you. Share the picture with the class and tell what you would do differently.

2. Draw and color a poster showing the four steps to help you handle a bully.

🧎 Role Play

Have students role play the following situations (direct the role play so that students practice the four steps in handling a bully).

1. On the bus, Joe threatens you and tells you have to move out of "his" seat.

2. Bill tells you he's going to beat you up if you don't carry his books.

3. Lori says she's going to have her big sister beat you up if you don't give her your Barbie.

4. Tom always pushes you out of line when it is your turn to kick when playing kick ball.

5. Jill tells you that if you don't let her copy your paper, she will tell all your friends not to play with you.

6. Ellen tells you that if you don't let her wear your new sweater, she will push you into a mud puddle.

7. Tom refuses to bring pencils to school because he can always take yours.

8. Your big brother makes you do the dishes when it's his turn or he will tell mom one of your secrets.

9. Bob, a fifth grader, spits on you.

10. Tori stops you on your way to school and demands your lunch money.

☑ Lesson 18
Handling Put-downs

> Handling put-downs — A put-down is anything that is said to hurt another. Handling put-downs means using ways to deal with those who use put-downs.

Handling put-downs takes the ability to think clearly without reacting in an emotional way. If you yell, cry, or return the put-down, this encourages the person doing the put-down because that is what they want you to do. You must always take the responsibility for what you say but you must remember you are not responsible for what the other person says. *It is not your problem, it is theirs. You're okay!* There are steps you can use to help you deal with those who use put-downs: (1) Ignore them (if possible) or use a come-back statement to stop them, such as "Big deal," "So what," "I agree." (2) Use positive self-talk and tell yourself that you know you're good at something specific, like addition, reading, spelling, drawing animals, riding a bike, or other things. (3) Tell yourself, "It's their problem, not mine. I'm okay."

Directions: Read introduction and discuss the steps to handling put-downs. Ask students what they have been learning about responsible behavior and have them name some examples. (Be a good listener, resolve conflicts peacefully, be kind and cooperative, and practice self-control.) Ask the students what responsibility has to do with handling put-downs. (It is our responsibility to take care of our own feelings and know what to do when we are being put down.) Teach the students the steps to handling put-downs. Do this by asking students, "What do you think is the very, very best thing to do when someone is putting you down?" (When students answer, "Ignore them," say ignoring them is absolutely the very best thing to do! Then ask what could happen if you both keep putting each other down? (Fight, get hurt, get in trouble, etc.) Tell them that if they just can't ignore the put-downs to chose a come-back statement that they can say that will stop the put-downs. (See suggestions above and in Appendix B; be sure students use one of those suggested. This will assure that students will not use come-back statements that are also put-downs.) For step 2, have students name some specific things that they are good at and list them on the board. Then, ask students whose problem it is when they get put down. (It is the problem of the person doing the put-down.)

If using puppets have students stand where they can be seen by the other students. Have them raise their puppets when they hear their character's name so that the other students can see who is talking. Tell the students to listen to the story to see how the animal friends handle put-downs.

The New Girl

Minnie Moo, Susie Squirrel, and Kathy Kat were excited at recess because they were going to get to play with the new student, Vicki Vulture, who came into Mr. Moose's room that morning. Vicki was from another part of the country and had never been to Anytown before her parents moved here last week.

"Hi," said Minnie as Vicki came up to the three friends.

"Hi, yourself," said Vicki. "What goes on in this little school, anyway? The school I came from was lots bigger."

Susie said, "We have lots of fun here at Sunshine Elementary. Do you want to play kick ball or swing with us?"

"I don't swing with babies. In my school we got to play real baseball, not that stupid kid kick ball," said Vicki with a superior tone of voice. "Don't you guys do anything but play baby stuff?" She looked at Susie and Kathy and as Kathy looked like she was going to cry, Vicki said, "Little babies, are you cry babies, too?" Then she looked at Minnie and said, "You are big enough to play real games if you wanted, fatso."

Susie and Kathy glared at Vicki and Minnie was getting angry but just then Lilly Lambkin came over. "Hi, guys, what are we going to do, swing or jump rope?"

"Another one! And this one is like a white fuzzy rug. Are you a rug?" Vicki said before anyone got a chance to answer Lilly.

Lilly looked at Vicki in astonishment but decided to ignore the put-down. Mrs. Giraffe had just been teaching how to handle put-downs and Lilly remembered the very best thing to do is ignore it. Susie, Kathy, and Minnie caught on fast since Mr. Moose had also been teaching about handling put-downs. The four friends walked over to their other friends getting ready to play kick ball.

Just then Cherry Chicken and Polly Pigeon came up to Vicki. "Would you like to join us playing kick ball," asked Cherry. "We would be glad to teach you how to play."

This angered Vicki who, after all, was from a much bigger school where all her friends were and everybody played fun games. "Hey, I don't need anyone to tell me how to play your stupid baby games, skinny feet."

Now Cherry had seen her four friends walk away from Vicki and figured out fast why they were ignoring what Vicki was saying. Cherry knew all the steps of handling put downs so she decided to use a come-back statement. She looked at Vicki and said, "Big deal." Then she grabbed Polly's hand and the two of them walked off, leaving Vicki alone. Cherry remembered the second step to do to take care of your feelings so she did some self-talk, saying to herself, "I am really good at drawing and playing hop scotch."

Polly had watched the whole thing and she recognized Cherry's come-back statement. Polly also remembered the third step to handling put-downs. She said to Cherry,

"That new girl must be having a really bad day. It's her problem, not ours." They walked off to join the others.

Vicki just stood there watching. "What a bunch of babies," she thought. "I really don't care what they are doing. I don't like this school anyway."

Then the recess bell rang and the students all went inside. Mr. Moose asked for the math assignment then said, "Let's review our lesson on handling put-downs. Remember, we were talking about how to handle a situation when someone puts you down and hurts your feelings. What is the very best thing to do?"

Susie raised her hand, "Ignore the put-down."

"Right, Susie. But what if you can't ignore them and just have to say something back?" asked Mr. Moose.

"Say a come-back statement like big deal," said Minnie Moo as she looked over at Vicki.

"The second step in handling put-downs is important, too. What is it?" asked Mr. Moose.

Kathy raised her hand, "Talk to yourself and say something you are really good at doing, like I can sing."

"Correct," said Mr. Moose. "But what is the final step?"

Corky Colt volunteered, "Remember that it is always the problem of the person doing the put-downs, not yours."

Vicki suddenly realized that in her unhappiness about being taken from her old school and coming to Sunshine Elementary, she had been acting silly. She had been putting down everyone she met here. No wonder everyone was ignoring her. She decided right then and there that she had better shape up or she could go through the whole year without making friends.

At afternoon recess, Vicki walked up to Polly and said, "I was being mean at recess. I'm sorry. I would like to learn how to play kick ball. Maybe tomorrow you guys can teach me. I promise to never again put you or your friends down. Can you forgive me? I know it was my problem because I'm new and I miss my old school."

Polly smiled and called the other friends over. "Vicki wants to learn how to play kick ball, shall we teach her? She's sorry she put us down." Then she turned to Vicki, "I know how hard it is to go to a new school because you miss your friends. I was new here earlier this year."

Cherry smiled and said, "Sure, but why wait until tomorrow. Let's go over the rules for kick ball now."

⚠️ Discussion Questions

1. What are put-downs? (Any talk that hurts another person's feelings)

2. Who was using put-downs? (Vicki)

3. How did Susie Squirrel, Kathy Kat, and Minnie Moo handle the put-downs? (Used Step 1, ignored the put-down.)

4. How did Cherry handle the put-downs? (Used a comeback statement and self-talk)

5. How did Polly handle the put-downs? (Used Step 3 by saying it was Vicki's problem, not hers.)

6. What make Vicki Vulture realize she was using put-downs. (They were reviewing handling put-downs in class.)

🏃 Activities

1. Have each student name a come-back statement and something they are good at doing. You might have the students write them down to be used in the role plays.

2. Tell about a time you were put-down and how you felt.

3. Tell about a time when you put someone down. How do you think they felt?

4. Have students draw a picture of how they would use the three steps to handling put-downs. Share with the class.

🧎 Role Play

When role playing, have the students use puppets so that students are not directly using put-downs on each other. Before starting, review steps to handling put-downs. Direct students to use the three steps to handling put-downs (see lesson introduction).

How would you use the three steps to handling put-downs if Vicki said . . .

1. You act like a baby.
2. When you sing you sound like a howling dog.
3. It looks like you borrowed your shirt from your grandmother.
4. You play baseball like a three-legged cow.
5. You look like you're wearing a Halloween mask all year.
6. You read like you are in kindergarten.
7. You run like a sissy.
8. You need to go on a diet.
9. You can't do anything right.
10. You are dumb.

☑ **Lesson 19**
Refusal Skills

> Refusal Skills — Refusal skills are skills that help you say "no." They also help you to have some control over your life and actions and saying "no" sometimes helps prevent you from getting into trouble.

Saying "no" is sometimes hard, especially when our friends are encouraging us to do something that sounds like fun or they make it sound so good that we really think we want to do it. Refusal skills involve the ability to know when a situation is wrong or has possible negative consequences and know how to handle it. Learning to use refusal skills is our responsibility. (1) Say "no" and name what it is you are saying "no" to. (2) Come up with another activity or change the subject. (3) Just walk away.

Directions: Review what students have learned this year about responsibility. (Be a good listener, resolve conflicts peacefully, be kind and cooperative, and practice self-control.) Ask students what knowing how to say no, using refusal skills, has to do with responsibility. (It is the student's responsibility to know how to say "no" to avoid getting involved in activities that will get them into trouble.) Tell the students to listen to the story so they will be able to tell if the princess was finally able to use refusal skills and stay out of trouble.

The Princess and the Dragon

Once upon a time, long, long ago, there was a beautiful young princess who was the daughter of King Atilla and Queen Rora, the rulers of the land of Madaton. The beautiful young princess, whose name was Adeena, was very spoiled and always got her own way. Her father, the King, and her mother, the Queen, could not say "no" to anything Adeena wanted, even if it was not altogether in Adeena's best interests. There was the time Adeena wanted her very own horse, which is not so surprising except that Adeena was only two and as everyone knows, it is difficult for a two-year-old to ride a horse. So, of course, an adult had to take her riding and Adeena soon tired of the horse.

By the time Adeena started school, she was known as a bit of a brat by the castle workers. Things weren't any better at school either. Both the teacher and the other students would get quite upset with Adeena because she always had to be the center of attention. The teacher had a hard time getting Adeena to listen and not talk when the teacher was busy teaching. And the other students, particularly Norman, had a hard time playing with Adeena because she always wanted to be the one to decide what game to play on the playground.

Now, Adeena was very smart as well as being very beautiful and very spoiled, so she passed first grade with "A's" in everything except citizenship where she earned an "F." Both the Queen and the King talked to Adeena and explained that she must learn to cooperate with others and that they were instructing the second-grade teacher to say "no" to Adeena whenever necessary. Also, they told her she could no longer order any of the other children to be put into the dungeon if they did not do what she wanted.

Second grade went better than first grade for the other students because Adeena was learning how to play with them. She would have fun at recess with the other students and learned to play many games, instead of only the ones she knew. In fact, she became known as ready to try almost anything and would take any dare, probably because she didn't know how to say "no" since no one had ever said "no" to her. She would tell the other students, "I am the princess and I can do anything."

Then one day, Adeena teased Norman and he got angry. He decided to dare the little princess to do a most foolish thing. He knew she would have to back down in front of the other students and then they would see she wasn't so great. So, Norman dared Adeena to go into the cave of Bufus, the big, fire-blowing dragon, and see the dragon's gold and jewels. Everyone in Madaton knew about the dragon's treasure and knew Bufus kept it in his cave which he rarely left. Everyone in Madaton also knew that if Bufus ever caught anyone in his cave, he would cook them like fried eggs with his fiery breath. The story goes that a long time ago one of the foolish youths of Madaton tried to steal some of Bufus' treasure but he never came back from the cave and a fried egg smell came from the cave entrance for two days after the youth had entered the cave. Since then no one has ever ventured into the dragon's cave and all the children were told to stay away.

"I double dare you to go into Bufus' cave and find his treasure," Norman repeated.

Adeena's friend, Mara, told her to ignore the dare or just say "no." But Adeena couldn't because she didn't know how to say "no." Then Mara suggested everyone go play ball but no one did. Mara said to Adeena, "Let's just go play on the swing."

But the beautiful princess didn't want to back down in front of the other students even though she was afraid of going into Bufus' cave because she didn't want to end up like a fried egg. So the little princess said to Norman, "No problem. I can do it."

Norman didn't let it go. He asked, "When?"

"Oh, tomorrow or some time," answered Adeena.

By now all the second graders had gathered around and they wanted to see if Adeena really would do it so Norman said, "Okay, then tomorrow it is."

Adeena realized she was trapped. "Okay, tomorrow."

"How will we know you were there?" asked Lou.

"She can bring back a piece of the treasure," said Norman. "Do you agree, Adeena?"

"Yes" mumbled Adeena, not happy about the whole thing.

That night Adeena had a hard time getting to sleep because she was worrying about going into Bufus' cave the next day. Finally, she went to sleep and suddenly it was the next day.

All the second graders and some of the first and third graders went to the mountain behind the school where the dragon lived in his cave. Someone said the dragon had flown away and Adeena was glad. Still she crept quietly up to the cave entrance and with one last look at the bright sun, slowly went in.

It was dark in the cave and Adeena knew she would have to go quite a ways to find the dragon's treasure. While she was walking she said to herself, "This is silly. Why am I in this cave hunting for treasure? I could get really hurt if the dragon comes back. I wish I had never said I would do this. What can I do?"

The little princess kept going, making many turns and going down and up many rock steps. After awhile she saw a glow in the dark. She ran toward the glow and then she saw it — the dragon's treasure. Much gold and many jewels were piled all around and the glow was coming from the treasure but, horrors! There was Bufus, sleeping on his treasure.

Adeena just wanted to turn around and run back to the entrance but she was stuck with her dumb words — that she would bring a piece of the treasure back to show she had been here. Oh, how she wished she would have known how to say "no" to Norman. What was she going to do?

Just then one gigantic eye opened and Bufus seemed to look right at her. Adeena ran and ran, even crying out. That was when she woke up and looked around her. She was still in her room and it was all a dream! That's when Adeena decided that the next day she would tell Norman "no." She wasn't going to be foolish and go into a mountain with a fire-blowing dragon. She thought, if I am going to be a queen, I need to practice being really smart and being really smart means sometimes saying "no." Then she thought, if he won't understand no for my answer I'll just walk away.

The next day, Norman came up to Adeena and said, "Okay, let's go up the mountain so you can go into the cave."

To Norman's surprise, Adeena said, "No, I'm not going to be foolish and go into the mountain cave of a fire-blowing dragon. That's silly."

Norman just looked at her. Then Adeena looked at him and the other second graders and said, "Let's all go to the castle and play hide-and-seek."

Everyone thought that was a good idea and off they went.

The King and Queen were talking to each other nearby when they heard what Norman said and Adeena's answer. "Is that our beautiful princess talking? Has she finally started to grow up and learn that we must make choices and be responsible for our choices? It sounds like she has learned that sometimes people should say "no," said the King proudly.

⚠ Discussion Questions

1. Describe Adeena. (She was the beautiful but spoiled daughter of the King and Queen of Madaton.)

2. What did Norman dare Adeena to do? (To go into the dragon's cave, find the treasure, and bring back a piece.)

3. Who tried to stop Adeena from taking the dare? (Mara) How? (Mara told Adeena to say "no," ignore the dare, go play ball, or swing.)

4. Why did Adeena take the dare? (She didn't know how to say "no" and she was afraid the other students would look down on her.)

5. What happened that night to change Adeena's mind? (She had a bad dream about going into the cave.)

6. What did Adeena learn? (She learned how to say "no" and named the activity that she was refusing to do because it was dangerous.)

7. What did Adeena do to take everyone's mind off the dare? (She suggested they all go to the castle and play hide-and-seek.)

🏃 Activities

1. Draw and color a picture of Bufus sitting on his treasure in his mountain cave.

2. The teacher reviews the three refusal skills. (1. Say "no" and call the activity by its real name; 2. Come up with another activity or change the subject; 3. Just walk away.) Then have each student draw a picture showing one of the three skills and explain it to the class.

3. Write a paragraph about a time you didn't say "no" when you knew you should have and describe what happened.

& Role Play

Show how you would use refusal skills if . . .

Guide students in using the three refusal skills.

1. Brent dares you to skip school with him the next day and go to the mall.

2. Sara dares you to jump off the top of the slide.

3. Ben wants you to steal a candy bar at the store when he does.

4. Jack and Jill want you to take a drink of their dad's beer while you are at their house.

5. You are staying at a friend's house and they want you to sneak out of the house and go play with them in the nearby park after dark.

6. Tammy wants you to try the cigarette she took from her mother's pack and dares you to smoke with her.

7. Barry and Ted want you to join them in picking on the new kid who talks differently.

8. Your sister borrowed your coat and lost it. Now she wants you to lie for her and tell your parents someone stole it.

9. Lindsey wants to copy your math assignment for school.

10. Charles won't take turns on the swing so Matt wants you to help push him off.

☑ Lesson 20
Making Good Choices

> **Making Good Choices** — Making good choices is the ability to choose appropriate actions or behavior when offered different selections.

We are faced with choices all the time in our every day life. We have to choose how much of our lunch we are going to eat, who to play with, what games to play, what clothes to wear, what toys we want, what kind of haircut we want, and make many other decisions. Life is full of choices even when we are young. It is our responsibility to learn how to make good choices because it will help keep us safe, have friends, get good grades, and make our family proud of us. Making good decisions is not always easy because we don't always know what makes some decisions good and others bad. Sometimes we make mistakes in our choices, but that is how we learn. The important thing is to take the responsibility to learn to make good choices so that when we grow up we can do it easily. The two questions to ask ourselves about possible choices are:

1. Will it hurt anyone?
2. Will it be breaking rules?

Directions: Read and discuss the introduction. Review what students have been learning about responsibility. (Do chores, take responsibility for our actions, take care of our feelings, be honest, cooperate, and practice self-control.) Ask students what responsibility has to do with making good decisions. (It is our responsibility to learn how to make good choices so when we grow up we can have the ability to make good decisions.) Guide students in determining that making good choices helps us keep ourselves and others safe, follow rules, and stay out of trouble. Review the questions students should ask themselves when they have a difficult decision to make. (Will this choice hurt anyone? Will this choice be breaking rules?) If using puppets, select students to hold up their puppets as the characters' names are mentioned. Tell students that in the following lesson, Lucky and Lilly Lambkin will have to make an important choice. Tell them to listen carefully to the story to find out if Lilly and Lucky make a decision that will put them in danger or one that will keep them safe.

The Gun

One rainy Saturday afternoon Mrs. Lambkin told Lucky and Lilly that she was going to go to Mrs. Parrot's next door and would be gone for about a half an hour. She asked them if they wanted to go and both said they didn't. "You are both seven years old so I guess you will be all right and you both are responsible enough not to break any rules. Here is Mrs. Parrot's phone number or run over if you want to."

"Oh, mom," said Lucky. "We will be fine. You can trust us."

"Mom, I'll take care of Lucky," said Lilly laughing.

"Who will take care of who?" said Lucky.

"Don't you two fight, now. Why don't you play a game?" Mrs. Lambkin said as she headed out the door. "Remember to call Mrs. Parrot if you need to."

After she left, Lilly said, "Do you want to play a game?"

"Sure," said Lucky. "There's nothing good on TV. Let's play police and bank robbers. You can be the bank robber."

"Forget that," Lilly said. "I'll be the policeman."

Lucky got out the toy space guns he had in his room, tossed one to Lilly and said, "Let's practice a shoot-out. You can be the policeman this time. I'll be a space cop next time."

"Varoom! Varoom!" sounded the pretend guns as the two raced behind the chairs and sofa in the living room until with a loud yell and dramatic collapse on the floor, Lucky pretended to be shot. Lilly sat down beside him and laughed. "You really took a long time to die," she said and added, "Okay, I'll be the space ship robber and you can be the space cop this time but let's go upstairs where we can run up and down the hallway."

With that, she ran up the stairs and turned at the top and said, "Lousy space cop, I'll get away to Mars today."

Lucky scrambled up the stairs and chased her down the hall. As she ran into their parents' bedroom, he followed. Then he just stopped and stood there for a minute, even though Lilly said, "Varoom, you're dead." Lucky just stood there.

"What's wrong with you?" Lilly asked.

"I know where Dad keeps his gun," said Lucky. "It's on the top shelf of the closet. Let's play with a real gun."

"That's dangerous," said Lilly horrified. "What if it went off? Remember mom telling us about the little girl who got shot when her friends were playing with her dad's gun."

"Don't be silly, it's not loaded. Dad keeps the bullets in a plastic bag in the chest," Lucky said.

"Did Dad tell you where the gun and bullets are?" asked Lilly still amazed.

"Nah. Remember when I was looking for the Christmas presents last year. I found it then," said Lucky. "After I found the gun, one time I was with dad when he was getting ready to go target shooting and I saw him take the bullets out of the chest. I won't put the bullets in, we'll just play with the gun. It is really neat."

"Lucky, that's scary," said Lilly. "We can't do that. We could kill ourselves."

"I told you it doesn't have bullets in it so how could we kill ourselves?"

"Don't you remember when Dad said one time that we should always consider a gun loaded and never play with it?" asked Lilly.

"We wouldn't hurt anyone," said Lucky.

"But we could," said Lilly. "Mrs. Giraffe said we are always making choices and two things we always have to ask are if our decision could hurt anyone and if we would be breaking the rules. Now, Lucky, if we played with the gun, we could hurt someone — you or me — and it definitely is breaking the rules. Neither mom or dad would want us to play with the gun. Dad always tells us not to even touch a real gun."

"Aw, you're no fun," said Lucky. "But, I guess you're right. Mr. Moose said the same thing about choices last week. So, okay, let's play. Get going, I'm after you. You're still the space robber."

Lilly said, "I'm tired of playing police and space robber. Let's get a board game out and play it."

"Okay," said Lucky and the two headed downstairs.

⚠ Discussion Questions

1. What dangerous choice did Lucky want to make? (Wanted to play with a real gun.)

2. Why would playing with a real gun be dangerous? (You can never be sure *any* gun is unloaded.)

3. What were the two questions Lilly asked when making the decision about the gun? (1. Will it hurt anyone? 2. Will it be breaking rules?)

4. Whose responsibility is it to make the best decision when you are offered choices? (You are responsible for the decisions you make.)

5. Should Lucky and Lilly tell their parents that they know where the gun is? (Opinion. Yes, their parents need to be made aware that the youngsters know where the gun is and that they made a good decision.)

🧎 Activities

1. Draw a picture of a time when you had to make a difficult choice and share it with the class.

2. Print on the picture the two questions to ask about making decisions.

🧎 Role Play

The teacher reviews with students the two questions to ask about making good choices: Will it hurt anyone? Will it be breaking rules?

Using the two questions, what choice would you make if . . .

1. You were told to come straight home after school, but you want to go to the mall with your friends.

2. Marci wants to take a candy bar at the store without paying for it while you are with her.

3. You want to keep your friend's sweater because it is pretty.

4. You didn't do your homework and Tom offered his for you to copy.

5. Linda wants you to go to her house after school and you can't get your mom on the phone to ask permission.

6. An older neighbor boy is babysitting your brother and you and he wants you to help him drink the beer in the refrigerator.

7. You are taking care of your little sister and Matt wants you to come across the street for just a minute and see his new toy.

8. You are playing hide-and-seek and Jon and you talk about hiding in the trunk of your mom's car.

9. Your friend, Jake, brought a knife to school.

10. Your mom's pills are laying on the kitchen counter and your sister and you talk about eating them because they look like candy.

☑ Lesson 21
Learning from Our Mistakes

Learning from Mistakes — To learn is to gain knowledge or information and a mistake is an error or accident that happens. Learning from mistakes is the ability to gain knowledge after an error or accident happens.

Everyone makes mistakes from time to time. Sometimes we seem to make a lot of mistakes, but that is normal when we are young because we are learning or gaining knowledge about life. Sometimes we make mistakes because we don't know any better and sometimes we know better but things just seem to happen. Each time we make a mistake, we learn from that mistake so that we can either not make it again or know how to handle it if it ever happens again. For example, it may be our responsibility to feed the family dog and because we get busy playing we may make the mistake of forgetting to feed it and everyone seems to get angry with at us. We can lie and say we fed the pet or it wasn't our job, but that would not be honest. We must admit our mistake and correct it if possible, then remember to not make the same mistake again. We might break something accidentally. When questioned, we might want to lie about it and say we didn't do it, but it is our responsibility to admit it and do what we can to correct it.

Directions: Read and discuss introduction. Review what students have learned about responsible behavior. Have students name some examples. (Do chores, take responsibility for our actions, take care of our feelings, be honest, cooperate, and practice self-control.) Ask students what responsibility has to do with learning from our mistakes. (It is our responsibility to learn from our mistakes so we don't make them again.) Emphasize that everyone makes mistakes but it's how we handle those mistakes that helps others trust us and helps us feel good about ourselves. Guide students into understanding how most of us often feel the urge to lie about our errors and accidents but that if we do lie, others would not be able to trust us and we would not feel good about ourselves. To learn from our mistake, we must take responsibility for making the mistake and try not to make the same mistake again. If using puppets, select students to hold up their puppets as the characters' names are mentioned. Tell the students to listen closely to the following lesson to find out what Billy Goat learns about handling his mistakes.

The Mistake

When Billy Goat got home from school, he was furious with his brother, Gordy. It all started that morning when Gordy wouldn't let Billy into the bathroom which caused

Billy to be late for school. The rest of the day went from bad to worse and all the while Billy blamed Gordy for his miserable time. He was still fuming about his brother, who was in sixth grade and always got his way, when the phone rang.

It was Gordy's baseball coach with an important message. He told Billy to be sure to tell Gordy that the time for the play-off game was changed from 7 p.m. to 6 p.m. that night and he should be there at 5:30 p.m. After he hung up the phone, Billy said to himself, "Forget that. I'm not telling Gordy anything. He can find out for himself. I'm tired of him thinking he's so great." Then Billy went out to play and forgot about the call.

At dinner that night, Mrs. Goat asked Gordy what time his game was. Gordy told her it was at 7 p.m. at the Anytime Park. Gordy was really excited about the game and told his folks, "This is an important game. If we win this one and the next two games, we have a chance for the championship."

Mr. Goat patted Gordy on the head and said, "Don't eat too much. You don't want to play on too full of a stomach, particularly since you are one of the team's pitchers."

"Yeah, you're right," said Gordy. "I can't eat much because I am so excited anyway. I have to be there about 6:30 p.m."

Billy thought, I should tell him about the coach's message but I'm not going to because he thinks he so great and he's always so mean to me. So Billy didn't say anything.

The family left for the park at about 6:15 p.m. and when they got there at 6:30 p.m., they saw Gordy's team already playing on the field. As Gordy ran up, his coach said, "Where have you been? The game's almost over. Didn't your brother tell you I called and left a message the game time was changed to 6 p.m.?"

Gordy said, "No, he didn't!" And under his breath, he muttered "I'll get Billy!"

At the next inning, coach put Gordy in to pitch but the score was already 8 to 3 in favor of the other team. Gordy did the best he could as did everybody on his team but they lost 10-5.

Billy felt bad when he watched Gordy's team lose and he knew he was in trouble. He decided he had better say something as soon as possible. Before Gordy came back to the stands where Mr. and Mrs. Goat and Billy were sitting, Billy started to say that he just remembered that the coach had called and changed the game time to 6 p.m. and he had forgotten to write it down.

Then Billy remembered what Mr. Moose said about learning from mistakes and that it is everyone's responsibility to admit when they make a mistake and try to correct it. Billy couldn't figure out anything he could do to make up for his mistake of deciding not to tell Gordy about the game change but thought he should be honest and admit his mistake. So he told his folks, "The coach called tonight after school and I didn't tell Billy that the game time had changed. I'm really sorry."

Mr. Goat was angry. "Why didn't you?" he asked.

"I got busy and I was angry with Gordy for always being so mean to me," said Billy.

Just then Gordy came to the stands, with his head hanging down and feeling really upset about losing the game. He turned to Billy and said, "Billy, coach said he talked to you on the phone and told you about the time change. Why didn't you tell me?"

"I don't really know. I should have but I was angry with you and then I got busy. I'm so sorry. I wish I would have written it down. I don't know what I can do to make it up to you," said Billy.

"There's nothing you can do," said Gordy. "You already did it."

Billy knew then that sometimes people make mistakes and there's nothing they can do to make up for it. The best they can do is take responsibility for their actions and learn from it. He knew he really loved Gordy and he was sorry he had caused Gordy to miss the first half of the game. He remembered the times Gordy helped him learn to play baseball and how patient Gordy was when he could hardly hit the ball.

Then Billy thought of something. "Gordy, does your coach still need a bat boy? I'd like to make it up to you so I want to be the bat boy for the rest of the season."

"I thought you didn't want to do it because you wanted to play with your friends," said Mrs. Goat.

"Well, yeah, but I really do feel bad and helping Gordy and his team seems more important to me now. Do you want me?" Billy said as he turned to Gordy.

"Sure," said Gordy. "We still have two games to play and we might still have a chance for the championship. You better be the best bat boy we've ever had, little brother! We'll be working you hard. I'm going to need lots of drinks of water!"

"I know," said Billy.

⚠ Discussion Questions

1. Why was Billy angry with Gordy? (He wouldn't let him in the bathroom.)

2. What mistake did Billy make and how did he feel? (He didn't tell his brother about the time change of the baseball game. Later he felt sorry.)

3. What happened when Billy didn't give Gordy the message? (Gordy was late for the game.)

4. What did Billy do? (He took responsibility and admitted his mistake.)

5. Could Billy correct his mistake? (No) Why? (The game was over.)

6. What did Billy do to try to make up for his mistake? (Offered to be bat boy)

7. What did Billy learn from his mistake? (He learned to take responsibility for his behavior and never make the same mistake again.)

🏃 Activities

1. Draw a picture of a time you made a mistake.
2. Share the picture with the class and tell what you learned.

🧎 Role Play

What would you do if . . .

1. You lost your sister's Mickey Mouse watch.
2. You stuck out your foot and tripped Ben.
3. You squirted Lori with water from the drinking fountain and got her wet.
4. You pushed Amy off the swing on the playground.
5. You were supposed to make jello for dessert but you didn't.
6. You were playing around after school and missed the bus.
7. You put your glass of milk on the edge of the table and it got knocked off.
8. You tore up your group's picture because you didn't like it.
9. You have a dance recital and you didn't practice.
10. You are supposed to bring cupcakes tomorrow and you didn't tell your mother.

☑ Lesson 22
Smoking Is Harmful

Smoking Is Harmful — Smoking is when someone inhales or draws the smoke into their lungs. Cigarettes and cigars are what most people use. They are made from a plant called tobacco. When someone inhales the smoke from a cigarette or cigar, they take into their body many poisons that can cause disease and illness.

When people smoke tobacco, they take into their bodies nicotine, tar, formaldehyde, carbon monoxide, and hundreds of other chemicals. Many of these poisons cause cancer, heart disease, and other health problems. Cigarette smoking also gives people bad breath, yellow teeth, and wrinkles. It is best to never start smoking because the chemical called nicotine is one of the most addictive. This means that once a person's body gets used to nicotine it craves it or needs it. It is our responsibility to always take pride in ourselves and never start smoking. Most kids start smoking because they think it's cool or want to be accepted by friends who smoke. It is important to know how to resist the pressure from friends who want us to start smoking. It is important to know that more and more kids are choosing not to smoke because they know the damage that it can cause to their bodies. Knowing how to resist peer pressure to smoke is part of our responsibility. This is when we can use our refusal skills. The best way to do this is to: (1) say "no, thanks." This shows that you really don't want all the bad things that come with smoking. Your friends will usually respect your decision. If they keep asking you to smoke, then to keep friends: (2) you can suggest doing another activity or change the subject. Finally, if you must: (3) you should know how to just walk away.

Discussion: Incorporate the above information in the lesson by discussing chemicals in cigarettes and cigars, health problems caused by smoking, and how smoking is addictive. Then discuss what responsibility has to do with refusing to smoke. (It is the students' responsibility to know some ways to avoid doing something they know is harmful.) Review refusal skills. If using puppets, have students hold up their puppet when they hear their character talking in the story so other students can see which animal is talking. Tell the students to listen to the story about our animal friends to find out what they learned about smoking.

Smoking

Lucky Lambkin was on his way to Anytime Park to meet Billy Goat and Doolee Dog and play one Saturday afternoon. When he got to the park, he walked under the big maple trees until he came to the jungle gym but he couldn't find either Billy or Doolee. He went past the slide and merry-go-round and went on the bike path for a while searching. He was getting a little upset because both Billy and Doolee had said they would be at the park playground. Then he spotted them standing under a big tree talking to two big kids from school.

"Hi," Lucky said as he walked up to the group.

"Hi," greeted both Billy and Doolee. "You know Tony and Jack from fifth grade," said Billy. "They say we can hang out with them."

"Yeah," said Tony. "We don't mind you little guys tagging along with us but you have to play what we want to play."

"What do you want to play?" asked Doolee.

"Let's play frisbee," said Jack and he ran backwards and threw his blue frisbee to Doolee. Doolee jumped up and grabbed at the frisbee but missed. Billy got it quickly and threw it whizzing back to Tony. Lucky got into the act as Tony threw it back and Lucky got it with a high jump. His throw was a little short and both Tony and Jack laughed. Tony ran up on the frisbee and grabbed it from the ground, sailing the frisbee high over the heads of the three second graders who all jumped desperately to get it but missed.

"Geez, you guys are too little to play a good game of frisbee," said Tony. "It's boring."

"Yeah," said Jack. "Let's do something exciting." He looked at Tony and grinned. "Hey, Tony, let's teach these kids a fun thing to do."

"All right! That sounds great," said Doolee. "What is it?"

"Shall we tell them?" Tony grinned.

"Sure. They've got to grow up sometime," Jack said as he and Tony sat down under a tree and started looking in their pockets.

The younger boys were all eyes. It was really something that two of the big boys were including them in their play and they could hardly wait to see what Tony was going to pull out of his pocket.

"Here, have a cigarette," said Tony to Doolee as he put one in his mouth and pulled out a lighter to light it. Jack did the same, offering a cigarette to both Lucky and Billy.

It was quite an honor to have big boys include them but Lucky thought to himself that he really didn't want to smoke because he knew all the bad things about smoking. He knew it might give him lung cancer and yellow teeth. Besides that, it smelled really

Second Grade, Lesson 22: Smoking is harmful

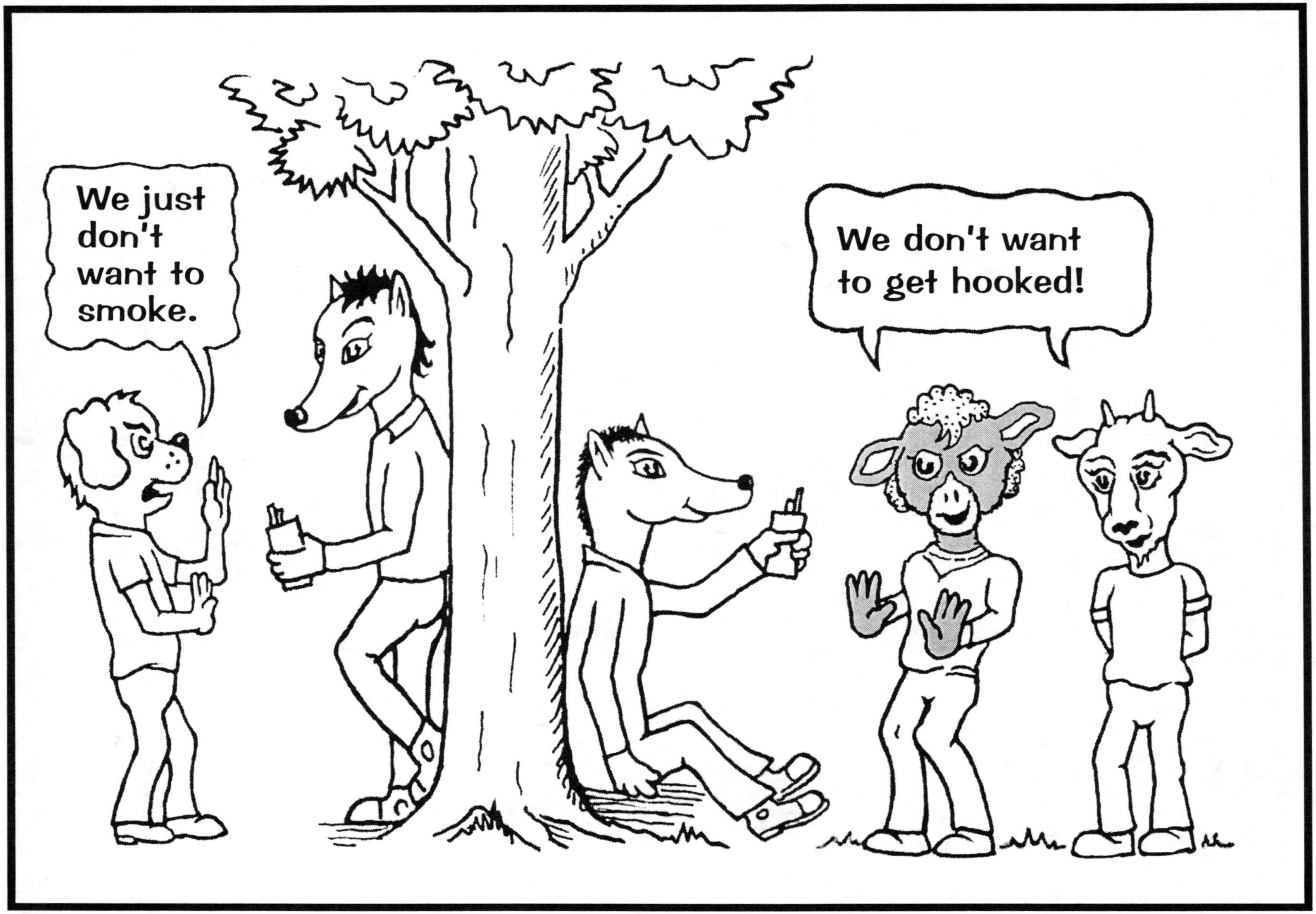

bad. He looked at Billy and Doolee who were just standing there too. None of the three young boys took a cigarette.

"Well, you want one or not?" asked Jack with a scowl. "Oh, maybe you're just too little to try something grown-up."

At that Doolee snarled and stuck his hand out to grab a cigarette, but then he said, "Naw. We're not too young. We just don't want to smoke."

Relieved that Doolee had said the words, both Lucky and Billy quickly added, "Yeah, we don't want to get hooked."

The two older boys took big puffs and both coughed. The three younger boys looked at each other and Lucky knew they were thinking of the refusal skills they had learned in school. Well, they had done the first one by saying "no" and now they needed to do the next one, thought Lucky. So he said, "Let's all go over to the baseball field. I bet we can get some other kids and get a game going. Come on, Billy and Doolee. Tony and Jack, you guys come, too."

"Geez, that sounds like fun," said Jack but Tony said, "Naw, it'll probably all be little kids like these two. Let's just sit and smoke for a while. Hey, kids, we may join you later."

"Okay," said Billy as he, Lucky and Doolee turned and ran toward the baseball field.

"Gosh, did you see how both of them coughed when they smoked?" asked Doolee. "I don't ever want to get a habit like that. What did the teacher call it?"

"An addiction," said Lucky. "Pretty soon your body craves it."

Just then they joined some other kids who were going to play ball.

⚠ Discussion Questions

1. Who did Lucky, Billy, and Doolee meet at Anytime Park? (Jack and Tony, two fifth graders)

2. What game did the five boys play? (Frisbee)

3. What did Tony and Jack want the three younger boys to do? (Smoke cigarettes)

4. How did Lucky, Billy, and Doolee handle the situation? (Doolee said he didn't want to smoke and Lucky and Billy said they didn't want to get hooked.)

5. What are the three refusal skills? (Say "no, thanks." This shows that you really don't want all the bad things that come with smoking. If they keep asking you to smoke, then to keep friends, you can come up with another activity or change the subject. Finally, if you must, you should know how to just walk away.)

6. How did Lucky, Billy, and Doolee refuse? (Doolee said no, Lucky suggested playing ball and all three boys walked away.)

7. Has anyone ever offered you a cigarette? If so, what did you do?

🎽 Activities

1. Make a poster showing some of the health problems from smoking.

2. Share the poster with the class.

🧎 Role Play

How would you handle the following situation if . . .

1. Your brother wants you to take Uncle Jerry's cigarettes.

2. Walking home from school your friend, Lisa, found part of an unsmoked cigar and wants you to put it in your mouth.

3. Shalee came over to play and pulled two cigarettes out of her pocket and wanted you to smoke them with her.

4. Your mom's friend left her cigarette burning in an ash tray and your friend, Jane, tries to talk you into puffing on it.

5. Rachel and you found an open pack of cigarettes and matches in the park and she wants you to smoke with her.

6. Dad was given a box of "sweet" cigars and your brother wants you to see if they are really sweet.

7. You visit Lori whose parents are smoking in the living room and the smoke makes you cough. (Guide students into realizing this is second-hand smoke and that they cannot tell the adults what to do but they can leave the room.)

8. When you won't smoke with your friend Jill, she wants to know why.

9. You and Dallas are looking in a magazine and see a funny advertisement about smoking. Dallas says it would be fun to smoke.

10. Cole, Braydan, and you find a container of chewing tobacco and Cole says, "Let's try some, it's not like smoking."

☑ Lesson 23
Alcohol Causes Problems

Alcohol Causes Problems — Alcohol is a legal drug that is in beer, wine, and liquor that can cause problems for the person who drinks it and the people around them. A problem is a matter that causes difficulty and needs to be worked out or corrected.

Because alcohol is a legal drug, only people who are 21 or older can drink it. If a person drinks alcohol before they are 21, they are breaking the law. When you turn 21, you can decide whether or not you want to drink alcohol. If you decide to drink it, it is important to learn to drink it responsibly so that it will not become a problem for yourself or others. You may decide not to drink alcohol at all.

When alcohol is in a person's body, it can affect their brain by making it slow down so walking, talking, thinking, and even breathing is changed. If the brain doesn't work right then the body can't work right either which often makes people act different from how they usually act. This can cause problems. A person who has been drinking alcohol may not be able to talk clearly and may stumble when they walk, even fall down, or get sick. That person may also become angry for little reason or may even become violent and try to start a fight or hurt someone. There is no way to tell how someone will act when alcohol is in their body. That is one of the reasons why drinking alcohol can be dangerous and cause problems. Drinking alcohol affects the person who drinks it and everyone around them.

People who drink can become addicted which means their body needs the drug, alcohol, to function. People who become addicted to alcohol are called alcoholics. The more they drink, the more their brain and body suffer and they lose control of their lives.

Sometimes youngsters try alcohol just to see what it is like and they may want you to try it, too. This is the time we must be responsible and use our refusal skills. The best way to do this is to: (1) Say, *"no, thanks."* This shows that you really don't want all the bad things that come with drinking alcohol. Your friends will usually respect your decision. If they keep asking you to "have a drink," then to keep friends, (2) *you can suggest another activity or change the subject.* Finally, if you must, (3) *you should know how to just walk away.*

Directions: Read and discuss introduction. Review what students have learned this year about responsibility and have them give examples. (Take responsibility for your be-

94

havior, practice self-control, have empathy for others, use problem solving, cooperate, be a good listener, and see both sides to a story.) Ask students what knowing about the dangers of alcohol has to do with responsibility. (It is the students' responsibility to know about the dangers of alcohol and how to avoid getting involved in situations that will get them into trouble.) Discuss the three ways to use refusal skills (listed above). Tell the students to listen to the story to see if the friends were able to refuse alcohol and stay out of trouble.

The Party

Billy Goat, Doolee Dog, Cherry Chicken, and Lucky and Lilly Lambkin were leaving the local mall where they had just attended the latest Disney movie. It was a bright, sunny Saturday afternoon and the friends were happily skipping along while discussing the events of the movie. Their parents would be picking them up at Billy's house since it was close to the movie theater.

"Looks like Gordy, your brother, is home," said Lucky as they walked up to Billy's front door.

"Yeah, mom and dad are out looking at new cars and Gordy promised to watch out for us until they get home about 5 o'clock," said Billy. "Looks like some of his eighth-grade friends are with him 'cause I hear them talking out back. Maybe they will want to play ball and we can play with them."

The youngsters were having a glass of juice when Gordy came in and said, "Hey, you guys want to come outside and have some fun?"

"What are you doing out there?" asked Cherry.

"Come on out and see," said Gordy with a funny looking grin as he headed back out to join his friends.

The second graders finished their juice and hurried outside to see what Gordy had been so mysterious about. Sure enough, there Gordy and his friends were huddled in a circle laughing and sounding like they were having great fun. As the youngsters went up to the three big kids, they noticed that they were passing around a bottle.

"Is that pop? Can we have some?" Billy asked his brother.

Gordy laughed as he looked at Bart Bull and Patty Parrot who giggled.

"Sure," said Patty as she passed the bottle of beer to Billy.

"Don't take it," said Cherry. "It's beer and we're too young to drink alcohol."

"Aw, come on," said Bart. "A little beer won't hurt you. It'll put hair on your chest. In fact, why don't all of you have a drink."

Billy hesitated then he said, "No, thank you. We're too young."

95

Lucky spoke up quickly, "You guys are too young to drink beer, too. It's against the law for people under 21 to drink alcohol."

"Yeah," Billy agreed. "Where did you get it, anyway?"

Bart said, "What a bunch of wimps. I got it from my home . . . the refrigerator, you know! My dad will never miss it. Come on, have a little drink with us."

When the five youngsters just stood there, the three big kids ignored them and kept drinking from the bottle. When that one was empty, Bart opened a sack and got another one out. He just threw the empty one over the fence into Mrs. Peacock's yard.

"You shouldn't do that," said Billy. "Mrs. Peacock is an old lady and it's hard for her to pick up things."

"Oh, shut up, little brother," Gordy said and started trying to climb the fence but he seemed to have trouble because he kept sliding down and giggling. By this time the other two eighth graders were rolling around on the grass laughing.

"Yo' are so-o-o sil-l-l-y," said Patty or at least that seemed to be what she was trying to say but it came out really slow and funny sounding.

Then Bart went over to the swing set and sat on one of the swings. He tried to swing but fell out and just lay there.

The five second graders just stood there and looked at the three older kids.

"It's just like teacher said," Lilly commented softly to her friends. "They are having trouble speaking and moving because of the beer."

Doolee had just been standing there watching the whole thing and finally he went closer to the others, "We need to just walk away. We don't want to do what they're doing, it's wrong."

The other four looked at him and Lucky said, "You're right." They started off except Billy hung back looking at his brother. "Come on, Billy," said Doolee but Billy went back toward his brother, saying, "Gordy, this is not like you. You shouldn't drink that stuff. Why don't we all play ball?"

"Shut up," yelled Gordy as his mood suddenly changed and he came at Billy with a mean look and raised his arm like he was going to hit his little brother.

Billy turned and ran into the house and said to the others, "That's not Gordy. He doesn't act like that. He loves me."

"You're right," said Cherry. "He's acting that way because of the beer. Let's go out front and play a game while we're waiting for our parents."

Just then the youngsters heard a car drive up and Billy said, "That's mom and dad. Gordy and his friends are really going to be in trouble. I'm glad I'm not in their shoes."

⟨?⟩ Discussion Questions

1. What do you think the parents are going to do when they come home? (Answers vary)

2. What did the eighth graders do that was against the law? (They were drinking alcohol.)

3. Did the second graders act responsibly? (Yes) How? (Go over refusal skills with students. (1) Say *"no, thanks."* This shows that you really don't want all the bad things that come with drinking alcohol. If they keep asking you to "have a drink," then to keep friends (2) *you can come up with another activity or change the subject.* Finally, if you must, know how to (3) *just walk away.*

4. How were the eighth graders acting? (Bart threw an empty bottle over the fence and Gordy tried to climb the fence but fell down. They were all giggling and Bart fell out of the swing. Then Gordy got really angry with Billy and was going to hurt him.)

5. Why did the eighth graders act that way? (They drank too much alcohol.)

6. Did the eighth graders practice responsible behavior? (No, they were breaking the law.)

7. Has anyone ever offered you a drink of alcohol? What did you do?

🏃 Activities

1. Draw a picture of what you would do if anyone ever offered you a drink of alcohol. Then share it with the class.

2. In groups, make posters of the various effects of drinking alcohol.

🧎 Role Play

Teacher reviews the three refusal skills and some of the problems related to drinking alcohol.

How would you practice refusal skills if . . .

1. Your older cousin wants you to help him break into your parents' liquor cabinet to steal whiskey to drink.

2. Your dad left an open beer on the kitchen counter and your friend, Fred, suggests that you and he drink it.

3. Shelly and you are looking in the refrigerator and see a bottle of something you think is pop but when you open it, it smells like beer. Sara says, "Let's try it since it's open."

4. Whitney, your baby sitter, asks you to drink with her.

5. Your dad's friend offers you a drink from his beer can.

6. Walking home from school, an eighth grader wants you to smoke with him.

7. Your older sister is having a slumber party and she said you could sleep with them if you don't tell your parents that they are drinking wine.

8. Your older brother wants you to help him steal a beer from the store and drink it with him.

9. Luke's older brother, offers Luke, Toby, and you a cigarette.

10. Your parents went to a movie and left you and your sister home and you sister wants the two of you to drink the wine in the refrigerator.

☑ Lesson 24
Drugs Are Dangerous

> Drug Abuse – Drugs are chemicals that can change
> how the mind or body functions. Some drugs can cause
> dangerous damage to the mind and body. Abuse means
> to misuse or use wrongly. Drug abuse is when chemicals are
> misused and can cause damage to the mind or body.

It is our responsibility to always take pride in ourselves and avoid abusing drugs that can cause damage to our minds or our bodies. Some drugs or chemicals are medicines prescribed by the doctor or given to us by our parents to help us get better if we are sick. Yet these same drugs can hurt us if they are misused. We should always be careful to take only what our parents give us of these medicines and never take them without permission or on our own. However, there are really dangerous drugs called *illegal drugs* that can cause serious damage to our minds and bodies and should never be used, even once. Illegal drugs are ones that can hurt us and are against the law to buy, sell, or use. Use of these illegal drugs can cause us to become addicted to them. This means if we take the drug, our body then needs the drug and feels sick without it. Someone who is addicted to a drug is called an addict and usually does poorly in school or work. An addict usually loses interest in normal things and doesn't take care of their body so they become sicker and sicker and sometimes even die. There is always the risk that an addict can die from an overdose (using too much of the drug). We should always remember that *drugs hurt us*. If a friend should ever ask us to use a drug and say that it will be "fun" or "cool," we should ask ourselves the question, "Would a real friend want me to hurt myself?"

Directions: Read and discuss the introduction. Briefly review what it means to practice responsible behavior and have students give examples. (Keep "special" feelings, play fair, be kind, practice anger management, use refusal skills, and know how to handle bullies.) Then discuss what responsibility has to do with abusing drugs. (It is our responsibility to take care of our body and mind and say no to using drugs.) Stress that drugs can hurt our minds and our bodies and even cause death. Point out that sometimes our friends ask us to use drugs. Go over the question, "Would a real friend want me to hurt myself?"

If using puppets, have students hold up their puppet when they hear their character's name in the story so other students can see which animal is talking. Tell the students to listen to the story about the second graders so they can tell what they learned about taking someone else's medicine. Point out one person's medicine can be a dangerous drug to another person and cause serious mind and body illness.

The Pills

Minnie Moo had two of her friends over to play one Saturday afternoon. Susie Squirrel and Kathy Kat had come over and the three girls were upstairs in Minnie's room playing with Minnie's birthday doll house and little doll family. They had the dolls go through a whole day and it was such fun.

Then Susie came back from the bathroom and said, "Look what I found." She held up a bottle that really rattled as she waved it around.

"Gee, that's my mom's pill bottle," said Minnie. "Where did you find it?"

"Oh, it was just sitting on the bathroom counter and I knocked it over. Lots of pretty little blue and red pills fell all over. I had to pick them up and put them back," said Susie. "But I'm not sure I got them all. Will you guys come back in and help me look?"

Both Kathy and Minnie went into the bathroom with Susie and right away Kathy found one on the floor. "Oh," she said. "They are pretty ones and look they come apart." She put her tiny finger into the powder and then licked it. "Why, it tastes pretty good."

"You shouldn't taste it," said Susie. "My mom says you shouldn't ever take anybody else's pills because they could make you sick."

"Do they make your mom sick?" asked Kathy looking at Minnie.

"No, she feels better and gets rid of her headache after she takes them," said Minnie. "Look how they come apart," said Susie. "The powder is in little plastic holders." She started taking more pills apart.

"You are making a mess," said Minnie. Then Minnie started drawing in the powder and even Kathy got into the act. They were having great fun. It was like making powder pictures.

"Come on," said Susie as she started to lick her finger again. "Let's all have a taste. Just a little bit can't hurt you and if it doesn't hurt your mother, Minnie, it won't hurt us. Don't be a couple of sissies. Are you guys scared to try something different?"

"Susie, don't be silly," said Kathy. "Remember what Mr. Moose taught us yesterday about drugs. He said other people's medicine can hurt us and even make us really sick. And trying to talk us into taking it isn't going to work. Mr. Moose said to always ask ourselves if a real friend would want us to hurt ourselves?"

"I'm a real friend. I would never want you to hurt yourselves," said Susie with a sorrowful tone in her voice. "And you're right. I shouldn't ask you to take someone else's medicine and I shouldn't either. I guess I never really stopped to think. I know better. Let's clean up this mess and take the pills down to your mother so she knows we found them."

"Okay," said Minnie with relief in her voice. "You're right. That's what we should do."

The three girls got busy, washed the counter, and took the pill bottle down to Mrs. Moo.

"Girls," Mrs. Moo said after they told her what they almost did, "I wish you would have told me right away but I'm proud you didn't take any of the pills and you were responsible enough to realize that they could hurt you. Those are my headache pills and they are quite strong. You all would have gotten really sick and I would have had to call 911. Your teacher is right. Drugs of any kind can be dangerous."

⚠ Discussion Questions

1. What were Susie, Kathy, and Minnie doing? (Playing with Minnie's doll house.)

2. What did Susie find? (She found some of Minnie's mother's headache pills.)

3. What did Susie want Kathy and Minnie to do? (She wanted them to taste some of the powder from the pills.)

4. What did Susie say to try to talk Kathy and Minnie into taking the powder? (She said they were sissies and afraid to be different.)

5. What did Kathy tell Susie? (She said that real friends didn't try to talk friends into using drugs.)

6. What did Susie, Kathy, and Minnie do with the pills? (Took them to Minnie's mother and told her about what they almost did.)

7. Has anyone ever tried to get you to take someone else's pills? What did you do?

🏃 Activities

1. Draw a picture of Kathy refusing the pills that Susie wanted her to try.

2. List five reasons why you should not abuse pills or drugs.

🧎 Role Play

What would you do in the following situation if . . .

1. You found two of your dad's pills on the counter.

2. Erica and you are walking home from school and you find a bottle of medicine laying on the sidewalk.

3. You have a headache and Jason wants to give you some pills he has in his pocket.

4. Cody came out of the drugstore and noticed a package of medicine in the trash.

5. You see your brother taking some of your dad's pills because he said he had a headache.

101

6. Your little sister is using the vitamins to make a sandwich (she put butter on a piece of bread and stuck the vitamins on it then folded the bread over them).

7. Your little brother wants to eat his vitamins like candy.

8. Mom asked you to bring her her stomach medicine. It was pink and smelled delicious.

9. You fell down and cut yourself and your friend wanted to put her dad's foot ointment on it.

10. You found some pills in your aunt's old purse and wanted to pretend you were sick.

☑ Lesson 25
Setting Goals

> Setting Goals — Setting goals is to plan for a future
> wish, desire, or thing that we want.

To set a goal means to work for something that doesn't just happen but requires desire and planning. It means to be able to look ahead and have a dream for the future. You might want to get to know someone better, make a new friend, learn to print better, read a book, get along better with a sister or brother, or hit the ball farther. During our lives we will have lots of dreams and goals. Some of them we can work on and have in a few days or weeks, like when we learned how to ride a bicycle. Other goals take a long, long time, like graduating from high school.

Directions: Read and discuss introduction. Review responsible behavior and have students give examples. (Take responsibility for your behavior, do your school work, be honest, be a good listener, and practice self-control.) Ask students what being responsible has to do with setting goals. (It is our responsibility to set goals for ourselves and help plan for our future, rather than just letting things happen.) Tell students that to make a goal happen, we must have a plan. This means we must name the goal and then figure out at least two things to do to get the goal. Tell the students to listen to the following fable so they will be able to tell which insect has learned to set a goal, plan for it, then work to achieve it.

The Grasshopper and the Ant

Early on a frosty fall morning, Ant arranged her stores of grain for the long, cold winter ahead. She was tidying neat piles of wheat, oats, and corn when Grasshopper happened to pass by her open door. Grasshopper peered in, amazed at Ant's full pantry.

"Please, Miss," began Grasshopper politely. "Could you spare a few kernels of grain?"

Now Ant looked up from her work and stared hard at Grasshopper.

"And what were you doing during harvest while I worked from dawn to dusk collecting food for the winter?" she finally asked.

"That, my friend, is easy to explain," answered Grasshopper. "I was singing sweet songs of summer, of course. Perhaps you heard my lovely chirping."

"Yes, indeed, I did," answered Ant. "And did you enjoy yourself as you chirped away the seasons?"

"Well, yes, as a matter of fact, I did," answered Grasshopper, feeling the chill of a fall wind.

"Then, surely you will understand what I must say to you now, sir," began Ant.

Grasshopper nervously rubbed his legs together.

"Since you sang all summer while I was planning for the freezing months ahead, it looks as if you will have to dance all winter just to catch up." With this, Ant slammed tight her pantry door and disappeared into her stores of grain.

All next winter, Grasshopper will wish he'd remembered two important words — *plan ahead.*

⚠ Discussion Questions

1. Which insect set a goal and planned for the winter? (Ant)

2. How did Ant achieve his goal? (He harvested and stored wheat, oats, and corn to have food for the winter.)

3. Did Grasshopper set goals or plan for the future? (No) Why didn't he? (He was busy having fun singing.)

4. How does your family plan for the future? (Various answers: Point out that parents have goals for their family and work to provide food, clothes, and housing and sometimes special vacations.)

🐜 Activities

Ask students to name some of their important dreams and goals. Tell them that often our dreams can become goals. The teacher will write some or all of the ideas on the board. Tell the students to think about one special dream or goal that is important to them.

1. Draw a picture of the goal you would like to achieve. (Students may use an idea from the board.)

2. Write the two steps to accomplish your goal. Use the goal from Activity 1. Make a plan to achieve the goal by writing down two steps you can do to achieve your goal. (For example, if the goal is to buy roller blades, then the student would write down two ways to earn money to buy them.)

Role Play

Tell students that to make a goal happen, we must have a plan. This means we must name the goal and then figure out at least two things to do to get the goal.

How would you take responsibility to plan for the following goals . . .

1. Learn to braid my long hair.
2. Learn a new song.
3. Read six books over the summer.
4. Set the table properly.
5. Make spaghetti and meatballs for dinner.
6. Learn to bat well in T-ball.
7. Run faster at play day next year.
8. Learn to swim this summer.
9. Learn to play a game on the computer.
10. Make a new friend this summer.

Appendix A
How to Make Sock Puppets

1. Teacher or students provide enough crew-type socks of the appropriate size to fit students' hands. Post pictures of the characters so students can see what they look like while making the puppets. It is recommended that each student have a sock to work with even if some characters are to be duplicated. Remember to have at least one black sock (for Lucky Lambkin), one yellow sock (for Cherry Chicken), one gray sock (for Ted Turkey), and several brown ones (for Doolee and Daisy Dog, Corky Colt, Susie Squirrel, etc.). The others can be white or various colors.

2. Students can either make the puppets in class or the teacher may ask them to do it at home. If made at school, the teacher should arrange to have some adult helpers present. Students should each have a special character for their puppet but should be made to understand that they may not always be using that character but will share and/or trade them with other students.

3. If making the puppets in class, it will take about an hour for puppet construction and the teacher should have the following materials available: various shades of ribbon and yarn for hair and hair ribbons; black paper or inexpensive "wiggle" eyes available at craft stores, red paint for mouths; yellow felt for beaks; white cotton for fur; string and florist wire (or pipe cleaners) for whiskers and ears; glue that will attach paper, etc. to socks; pins to attach items to socks; and textile paint or fabric for making features.

4. Assign students a character. They should put a sock on one hand and determine where the face will go and have the teacher or adult helper mark it. Remember, mouths will have upper and lower jaws or beaks as students use their thumbs for the lower jaw and fingers for upper jaw. Students should cut out facial features from the paper (or they may use paint or markers to make the features). To see how the features look, teacher or adult helper pins them on the socks. Then students glue features in place, coloring with paints or markers as necessary.

5. Most characters' ears can be made by squeezing some of the sock into the proper shape and tying with string or gluing pipe cleaners on socks. Rabbit ears can be made using pipe cleaners or florist wire and gluing white paper to the wire before anchoring it to the sock.

6. Students pick appropriate ribbons, yarn, or cotton for hair. Ribbon may be curled using scissors (like curling ribbon for wrapping presents). After "hair" is glued on, ribbons or tiny paper or felt hats may be glued onto hair.

7.   Students may be creative in depicting their characters and add more color or innovations to their puppets. A main consideration is that the puppets be sturdy as they need to be stored at school and usable for many lessons. At the end of the year, students may want to take their character puppets home.

Appendix B
Resource Sheet 1

"I Am Special" Song
(Sing to "Brother John" tune)

I am special.
I am special.

So are you.
So are you.

Always remember
Always remember

This is true.
This is true.

Appendix B
Resource Sheet 2

"I" Message Formula

I feel _____

when _____

because _____.

Give examples how "I" Messages fit into the formula (i.e., I feel *hurt* when *you don't talk to me* because *I think you don't like me*. I feel *sad* when *you won't let me play* because *I don't have anyone to play with*.)

Appendix B
Resource Sheet 3

Win-Win Problem-Solving Guidelines

1. If you are angry, take three deep breaths and count to 10.

2. Each person states the problem. (No interrupting, name calling, or physical contact.)

3. Brainstorm solutions (together).

4. Choose a solution that is fair to all parties (win-win).

5. Follow through with the solution.

Appendix B
Resource Sheet 4

Come-Back Statements

Be sure students chose a come-back statement that they will remember and say. Have students chose from statements in Lesson 18 or from the list below to assure that students will not use come-back statements that are put-downs.

- Big deal.
- So what.
- I agree.
- See ya' . . .
- That was supposed to be a secret.
- How did you know . . .
- Tell it to my lawyer.
- Can you put that in writing.
- I disagree.
- You're probably right.
- Who told you . . .
- Oh, really?
- Okay.
- Are you sure . . .
- If you say so.

Appendix C
Responsibility Contract

To be signed after the second-grade curriculum has been taught.

    I, _____, am committed to learning how to be a kind, considerate, and responsible person by learning to do the following things:

- I will always remember I am special.
- I believe everyone is special and will listen to what they say and give them respect.
- I will be a good friend.
- I am honest.
- I try to solve problems peacefully.
- I can cope (make do) with whatever I need to do.
- I am always ready to learn.
- I try to make good choices and decisions.
- I have goals and work on them.
- I will be responsible for my own behavior, even when I make a mistake.

_____
Student's signature   Date

_____
Parent's signature (optional)   Date